WHO DO YOU SAY THAT I AM?

WHO DO YOU SAY THAT I AM?

When Jesus Is Not Who You Think

JOHN T. SEAMANDS

Beacon Hill Press of Kansas City
Kansas City, Missouri

Library of Congress Cataloging-in-Publication Data

Seamands, John T.
    Who do you say that I am? : when Jesus is not who you think / John T. Seamands.
        p. cm.
    Includes bibliographical references.
    ISBN 0-8341-1851-3 (pbk.)
        1. Jesus Christ—Person and offices. I. Title.
BT202.S385 2000
232—dc21

99-086118

10   9   8   7   6   5   4   3   2   1

CONTENTS

INTRODUCTION

The Christian faith centers on Christ—not a system of theology or ethics, not a creed or a ritual, but a Person, a unique Person. He is what makes the gospel different from religion or spirituality in general. Religion places emphasis on a person. Religion offers a system of thought, a set of teachings, and says, "Study these. Believe and follow these." By contrast, the gospel presents a Person and says, "Accept Him. Believe and follow Him."

Of course, the Christian faith does have its wonderful teachings, its lofty ethics, its system of theology, its rituals and creeds. But it is more than this. The Christian faith is *Christ* and is what it is because He is who He is.

In all the man-made religions of the world, there is no intrinsic relationship between the founder of the religion and the religion itself. You can take away the founder, and the religious system with all its major concepts remains intact.

However, take Christ out of the Christian faith, and you have *nothing* left. To be a Christian is not simply to join an organization, subscribe to a particular creed, or perform certain rituals. To be a Christian is to believe in Christ and to maintain a day-by-day relationship with Him.

Recall the story of Charles Colson, a member of United States President Richard Nixon's cabinet. "Chuck," as he was popularly called, was reputed to be a ruthless, hard-hearted "hatchet man." He became involved in the infamous Watergate scandal and was sentenced to prison for a short term. While incarcerated, he confronted the claims of Christ and surrendered his life to the Savior. As a result, Colson's life changed completely. The hard-hearted hatchet man of the White House became a compassionate helping hand of God's kingdom.

For many years now, Colson has been an effective nationwide evangelist with an especially effective and fruitful ministry among the inmates of America's prisons. Before his conversion, if someone had asked him, "What's your religion?" he would no doubt have answered, "I'm a Christian." But it was not until he believed in the person of Jesus Christ and came into a personal relationship with Him that his life was changed and took on special meaning.

Christ makes all the difference in the world. He has done something *for* us and can do something *in* us that no one else can do.

This book is written to enable the reader to reflect on the person of Jesus Christ, in addition to His miracles and parables. The latter, His works and teachings, grow out of His Personhood. We don't believe in Christ just because He performed miracles; we believe in the miracles because of who Christ is. He is a miracle himself—God in human flesh—so we would expect Him to perform them.

We don't believe in Christ because of His marvelous teachings; we believe in His teachings because of who He is. He is the truth, and so His teachings are unquestionably true.

Those who read this book should do so thoughtfully and prayerfully, asking such questions as

Who is this Person, Jesus Christ?

What has He done *for* me?

What can He do *in* me?

Do I know Christ? Am I in fellowship with Him?

How can I follow Him in my daily life?

May God bless you as you begin this adventure with the living Christ.

PART 1

The Person of Jesus Christ

E. Stanley Jones once wrote a letter to Mahatma Gandhi. "You know my love for you," he wrote. "I have tried to interpret you and your movement to the West. I had thought you had grasped the center of the Christian faith, but I'm afraid I will have to change my mind. You have grasped certain principles, which have molded you and made you great. But while you have grasped the principles, I feel you have missed the Person. You said in Calcutta that you did not turn to the Sermon on the Mount for consolation, but to the Bhagavad-Gita. Neither do I turn to the Sermon on the Mount for consolation; I turn to this Person, who embodies the Sermon on the Mount but is much more. Here I think you are weakest in your grasp: You've grasped the principles, but you have missed the Person. May I suggest that you penetrate through the principles to the Person and then come back and tell us what you have found?"

Mr. Gandhi wrote back and thanked Dr. Jones for his concern but then sidestepped the issue.

Stanley Jones was right. The center of the Christian faith is Christ, and to be a Christian is to believe in Him and come into fellowship with Him. Like Mahatma Gandhi, many others have not proceeded beyond the principles to the Person, so they have missed the joy and power that are inherent in the Christian life. Thus we begin our quest by centering on the Person of Jesus Christ himself.

1

WHO IS HE?

Scripture passage: Matt. 16:13-18

> When Jesus came into the region of Caesarea Philippi,
> He asked His disciples, saying, "Who do men say that I, the
> Son of Man, am?"
> So they said, "Some say John the Baptist, some Elijah,
> and others Jeremiah or one of the prophets."
> He said to them, "But who do you say that I am?"
> And Simon Peter answered and said, "You are the Christ,
> the Son of the living God."
> Jesus answered and said to him, "Blessed are you, Simon
> Bar-Jonah, for flesh and blood has not revealed this to you,
> but My Father who is in heaven. And I also say to you that you
> are Peter, and on this rock I will build My church, and the
> gates of Hades shall not prevail against it."

Key verse: "Who do you say that I am?" (v. 15).

Jesus' strategic question "Who do you say that I am?" is one every one of us must ask. It is a personal and universal question. Everything depends on our answer. Our relationship to Him will be largely determined by our attitude toward Him.

Who is Jesus anyway?

Is He Just a Man?

At the beginning of His public ministry when Jesus came back to His hometown, Nazareth, the people said to each other, "Isn't this the carpenter's son? Isn't his mother's name Mary, and aren't his brothers James, Joseph, Simon and Judas? Aren't all his sisters with us? Where then did this man get all these things?" (Matt. 13:55-56, NIV). Notice the phrase "this man." They looked on Jesus as an ordinary man.

On another occasion, while speaking to the Pharisees, Jesus asked the same question: "What do you think about the Christ? Whose Son is He?" The Pharisees responded, "The Son of David" (22:42). Again, they thought of Him only as a man, even though a man with royal blood in His veins.

Yes, Jesus certainly was man, every inch a man. He was born as a baby and lay in a manger. He grew up as all human beings have to grow—from childhood to adolescence to adulthood. He worked at a carpenter's bench with hammer and saw, plane and chisel. He went through the whole gamut of human experiences. He walked on our footpaths, slept on our hillsides, met our sorrows and temptations, suffered our hunger and thirst. He identified himself with our humanity (in the manger), with our toil (at the carpenter's bench), with our poverty (in that He had no place to lay His head), with our temptations (in the wilderness), with our sin (on the Cross). He met life as a human being, with no greater resources than we have at our disposal. He prayed, died, and was laid in a tomb. He was so human that He was called "the Son of Man." We feel He is so much like us that we want to put our arm around Him and call Him "brother man." But just then He steps in front of us and commands, "Come, follow Me." He is so much like us, and yet so much unlike us. He is a man all right, but so much more than a man!

Is He Just a Teacher?

A man by the name of Nicodemus called on Jesus one night and said, "Rabbi, we know that You are a teacher come from God" (John 3:2). Again and again we read in the Gospels that Jesus went about teaching the people. Yes, Jesus most certainly was a teacher, a wonderful teacher. His teaching was so remarkable that it is recorded, "The people were astonished at His teaching, for He taught them as one having authority, and not as the scribes" (Matt. 7:28-29).

The teaching of Jesus was remarkable for its *simplicity*. He spoke in down-to-earth language—in stories and parables. He talked about commonplace things and everyday experiences. He talked about the flowers, about the birds, about seeds and harvest, about lost sheep and runaway boys.

His teaching was remarkable for its *profundity*. Theologians and scholars are still trying to probe the depths of His revelation and truth.

His teaching was remarkable for its *purity of ethics*. Jesus equated hatred with murder, lust with adultery. He proclaimed not only right action but also right attitude and motive. He set a standard of holiness so high that it is unattainable by human goodness alone.

Finally, His teaching was remarkable for its *revolutionary stance.* He said, "Love your enemies, bless those who curse you" (5:44). If followed, His teachings would absolutely transform society and every individual.

The whole world recognizes Jesus as a great Teacher. We need to sit at His feet and learn from Him. He certainly *is* a remarkable teacher. But He's *much more* than a teacher!

Is He Just a Prophet?

When Jesus asked His question to the disciples, they answered, "Some say John the Baptist, some Elijah, and others Jeremiah or *one of the prophets*" (Matt. 16:14, emphasis added). At the time of His triumphal entry into Jerusalem, "all the city was moved, saying, 'Who is this?' . . . the multitudes said, 'This is Jesus, the *prophet* from Nazareth of Galilee'" (21:10-11, emphasis added).

When the Pharisees questioned the blind man whom Jesus had healed, they asked, "What do you say about Him because He opened your eyes?" He answered, "He is a *prophet*" (John 9:17, emphasis added).

When the woman at the well of Sychar met Jesus, she said to Him, "Sir, I perceive that You are a *prophet*" (4:19). And Jesus referred to himself as a prophet when He said, "A prophet is not without honor except in his own country and in his own house" (Matt. 13:57).

If there ever was a mighty prophet who declared the message of God and prophesied the future, it was Jesus. Even our Muslim friends are willing to go this far and recognize Jesus as a mighty prophet. But He is *more* than just a prophet.

Who Is He Then?

Jesus is more than man. He is God! As man, He was born in a manger; as God, He was worshiped by the wise men. As man, He suffered the pangs of hunger; as God, He spread a feast for 5,000 and had bread and fish to spare. As man, He was thirsty and asked for water to drink; as God, He said, "Whoever drinks of the water that I shall give him will never thirst" (John 4:14). As man, He was tired and fell asleep in a boat; as God, He arose and stilled the tempest. As man, He wept at the tomb of His friend Lazarus; as God, He said, "Lazarus, come forth!"

As man, He was tempted in all the ways we are; as God, He lived a sinless life. As man, He was crucified, was dead, and was buried; as God, He arose from the dead and lives forevermore.

Listen to the astounding claims that Jesus made:

"I am from above" (John 8:23).

"Before Abraham was, I AM" (John 8:58).

"I am the bread of life" (John 6:35).

"I am the light of the world" (John 9:5).

"I am the resurrection and the life" (John 11:25).

"I am the way, the truth, and the life" (John 14:6).

"I am the Son of God" (John 10:36).

"I am the Alpha and the Omega, the Beginning and the End" (Rev. 1:8).

"I am the First and the Last" (Rev. 1:17).

These are amazing claims! No person in the history of the world has ever claimed so much. Let it be noted—the uniqueness of Christ is not something that we Christians claim for our Master; this is what He claims for himself. His uniqueness is not something we *concede* to Him, but something that He *confronts* us with.

Jesus is either who He claims to be, or He is not. There is no middle ground. He is either the greatest deceiver—the biggest liar—this world has ever seen; or He is exactly who He claims to be. And countless millions of people of all races, of all walks of life, living in various generations have taken Jesus at His word and found Him by personal experience to be all He claims to be. If Jesus is not who He claims to be, nothing matters. If He *is* who He claims to be, nothing else matters.

Jesus is more than teacher and prophet. He is Redeemer, Savior! The angel said to Joseph, "You shall call His name JESUS, for He will save His people from their sins" (Matt. 1:21). The angel who appeared to the Bethlehem shepherds announced, "There is born to you this day in the city of David a Savior, who is Christ the Lord" (Luke 2:11). Addressing the Sanhedrin, Peter said of Christ, "Him God has exalted to His right hand to be Prince and Savior, to give repentance to Israel and forgiveness of sins" (Acts 5:31). Paul said of Him, "This is a faithful saying and worthy of all acceptance, that Christ Jesus came into the world to save sinners" (1 Tim. 1:15).

We are all born sinners, and therefore we need more than just a teacher, an example, or a prophet—we need a Redeemer.

Our Hindu friends will come so far. They will agree that Jesus is divine. But they claim He is only *one* of many incarnations and one of many saviors. He is *a* savior, but not *the* Savior.

What does the Word of God say on this subject? "Nor is there salvation in any other, for there is no other name under heaven given among men by which we must be saved" (Acts 4:12). "There is *one* God and *one* Mediator between God and men, the Man Christ Jesus, who gave Himself a ransom for all" (1 Tim. 2:5-6, emphasis added).

What does Jesus himself claim in this regard? He says, "I am the way, the truth, and the life. No one comes to the Father except through Me" (John 14:6). "I am the door of the sheep. All who ever came before Me are thieves and robbers, but the sheep did not hear them" (10:7-8). So the Bible declares, and Jesus himself claims, that He is the *only* Savior of humanity. The blind man who was healed by Jesus first saw a prophet and then the Christ (see 9:17, 38). The sinful woman at the well of Sychar first saw a man, then a prophet, and finally the Christ (see 4:9, 19, 29). When confronted by our Lord, Peter declared, "You are the Christ, the Son of the living God" (Matt. 16:16). And Thomas, when he saw the resurrected Christ, confessed, "My Lord and my God!" (John 20:28).

The Lord Jesus Christ stands before you today and asks that same eternal question: "Who do *you* say that I am?" What will your answer be? A good man? A remarkable teacher? A great prophet? Or wonderful Savior?

2

WHAT SHALL I DO WITH HIM?

Scripture passage: Matt. 27:11-17, 21-24

Now Jesus stood before the governor. And the governor asked Him, saying, "Are You the King of the Jews?"

So Jesus said to him, "It is as you say."

And while He was being accused by the chief priests and elders, He answered nothing. Then Pilate said to Him, "Do You not hear how many things they testify against You?" And He answered him not one word, so that the governor marveled greatly.

Now at the feast the governor was accustomed to releasing to the multitude one prisoner whom they wished. And they had then a notorious prisoner called Barabbas. Therefore, when they had gathered together, Pilate said to them, "Whom do you want me to release to you? Barabbas, or Jesus who is called Christ?" . . .

They said, "Barabbas!"

Pilate said to them, "What then shall I do with Jesus who is called Christ?"

They all said to him, "Let Him be crucified!"

Then the governor said, "Why, what evil has He done?"

But they cried out all the more, saying, "Let Him be crucified!"

When Pilate saw that he could not prevail at all, but rather that a tumult was rising, he took water and washed his hands before the multitude, saying, "I am innocent of the blood of this just Person. You see to it."

Key verse: "What then shall I do with Jesus who is called Christ?" (v. 22).

We have already stated that the basic question in the Christian faith is "Who is Jesus?" And we discovered that He is more than a great man, a great teacher, or a great prophet. He is the divine Son of God, the Savior of the world.

Having answered this basic question, we are immediately faced with a second important question, the same question that Pontius Pilate asked almost 2,000 years ago: "What then shall I do with Jesus who is called Christ?" The two questions are inseparably related, for if Jesus is truly the Savior, then our response to Him as a Person is a matter of life and death.

First let us recall the context in which this question was asked.

This is one of the most dramatic incidents in the life of Jesus. It is filled with intense action and deep emotion. Here stands Jesus on trial before the Roman governor, Pilate. What a scene of contrasts! Pilate is seated on a marble throne, surrounded by his personal bodyguard in a beautiful hall resplendent with the glory of Roman architecture. He is dressed in his fine toga and mantle—a man with good intentions but a weak will.

Before him stands Jesus, the sinless Son of God, dressed in a common toga but neat and immaculate. There is a dignity and radiance about His bearing that commands the attention and respect of all in spite of His enemies' deep hatred for Him. They become a howling, stampeding mob, enraged with a murderous hate and a bestial lust for revenge.

At the height of the excitement, when the tension is greatest, Pilate suddenly raises his hand and quiets the tumultuous crowd. Then amid a deathly silence he asks this momentous question: "What then shall I do with Jesus who is called Christ?"

Jesus' accusers cry out incessantly at the top of their voices, "Away with Him! Crucify Him—crucify Him!"

This scene has been reenacted down through the centuries in the lives of untold millions of individuals. Jesus has been on trial before men, women, boys, and girls. And He's on trial today. *You* are in Pilate's chair today wearing the garments of sin and self-righteousness. Jesus, the spotless Son of God, stands before you wearing the garments of mercy and compassionate love. The world around cries out, "Away with Him! Crucify Him—crucify Him!" The decision lies with you. Jesus is on your hands. You're asking the question, "What shall I do with Jesus who is called Christ?" You have the power to reject Him or accept Him. All eternity depends on the answer.

Please notice three things about this question:

It is a personal question. What must *I* do? Pilate tried to shift the responsibility to the mob. When he found he couldn't change the mind of the people, he had his servants bring in a basin of water and washed his hands before them all, saying, "I am innocent of the blood of this just Person." But he failed to realize that the blood of a rejected Christ goes deeper than the power of water to cleanse. He washed his hands with water, but his heart was still unclean.

Pilate was just as guilty of the death of Christ as the Jewish rabble. He could have broken up the whole affair and saved Christ from death. The trial was illegal, the witnesses were false, and the prisoner was innocent. With one word he could have dismissed the trial, but he gave Jesus up to the mob and thereby became an accomplice in the Crucifixion.

Many people today are trying to shift the burden of responsibility onto someone else. Many say, "Everyone else is doing it—why not me?" But even if everyone else in your city rejected Christ, *you* would still be responsible for what *you* personally do with Him. Others might say, "If my husband [wife] would accept Christ, so would I" or "If my friend would accept Christ, so would I." But still you cannot escape the responsibility. This is a personal question demanding a *personal* answer. No one can answer this question for you; you must do it yourself. You can either reject Him or accept Him—there is no middle ground.

It is a pressing question. What *must* I do? Pilate had to make an immediate decision. He couldn't wait and ponder the matter. Jesus was on his hands. The people demanded an immediate answer. Something had to be done then and there. And so Pilate made his decision.

This question demands an immediate answer of you today. To try to postpone the decision is merely to make a decision against Christ, for there is no middle ground. It is either *for* or *against*. Again, to postpone the decision only makes an affirmative decision in the future more difficult. Every time you do this, you are establishing a set of mind, an attitude of the soul, that makes future rejection more certain.

It is a paramount question. Pilate washed his hands and thought the whole affair was closed. But nothing could erase the guilt of his heart. He had crucified Christ. He had set the course of his life; he had settled the destiny of his soul. History tells us that he came to a tragic end, that he took his own life to "end it all." The end of life of any person who rejects Christ is always tragic!

Everything depends on the decision you make. If you reject Christ, if you crucify Him afresh, your life will be without purpose, without peace and joy, without victory. If you accept Him as your Savior, your life will be radiant, joyous, and triumphant. Rejection means spiritual death; acceptance means eternal life.

One day the scene will be changed. Christ will be on the judgment throne, wearing the royal robes of kingship. You will be on trial before Him, for the Word says that "each of us shall give account of himself to God" (Rom. 14:12). On that day the question will be, "What will *He* do with *me?*" And the answer will depend on the answer you give now to the question, "What will I do with Christ?" If you reject Him as Savior here, on that day He will have to say, "I never knew you; depart from Me" (Matt. 7:23). But if you accept Him as Savior here, on that day He will say, "Enter into the joy of your [L]ord" (25:21, 23).

Jesus is on your hands. What will your decision be?

You can make one of three different responses to this question:

You can try to put Him *away.* Actually, putting Christ away is impossible. Herod tried to kill the baby Jesus but failed. Satan tried it. He did his best to tempt and sidetrack the Master, but he failed. The people tried it; they nailed Him to a cruel cross and laid Him in a tomb, but death and the grave could not hold Him. On the third day He arose from the tomb and was on their hands again. We may try to put Him away, but it is of no avail, for the Master is ever before us. He is inescapable.

You can try to put Him *off.* Some may try to put the Savior off; that is, they intend to make a decision in His favor someday, but not today. Like Felix the governor, they seek to put off the day of salvation to some more "convenient" day (see Acts 24:25). But this is exceedingly dangerous, for the longer we delay, the harder it becomes to accept the Master. Delay serves only to dampen our desire and harden our hearts.

John R. Mott, well-known lay evangelist for the Young Men's Christian Association (YMCA), once conducted a survey with an audience of 1,000 people. He questioned them as to what period in their lives they had received Christ as their personal Savior. Below the age of 20 years, 548 people responded; between 20 and 30 years of age, 337 people; between 30 and 40, 76 people; between 40 and 50, 15 people; between 50 and 60, 3 people; and over 70, only 1 person. That is, more than half of the audience accepted Christ when they were under the age of 20. Youth is the time of decision. This is the day of salvation; don't seek to put off the Savior. It may be too late.

You can try to put Him *aside.* Others try to take the name and teachings of Christ but not the Person of Christ himself. They admire the matchless teachings of the Master and want to put His principles into practice, but they don't want to receive Christ himself into their hearts and lives. This is an impossible position, for no one can live the life of Christ without His presence and power. It is only when He is living within us and working out His salvation through us that we can live up to the high standard He has placed before us. As we have already seen, the Christian faith is not merely a set of principles or a system of thought but a *Person*—it is what it is because *He* is who *He* is. When you accept Christ as a person, then you accept His commandments, His teachings, His example, and all that is connected with Him.

Put Him *On*

"Putting Christ on" is the scriptural response to the big question. The apostle Paul admonishes us, "Therefore let us cast off the works of darkness, and let us put on the armor of light.

"Let us walk properly, as in the day, not in revelry and drunkenness, not in licentiousness and lewdness, not in strife and envy.

"But *put on the Lord Jesus Christ,* and make no provision for the flesh, to fulfill its lusts" (Rom. 13:12-14, emphasis added). Jesus himself declares, "If anyone desires to come after Me, let him deny himself, and take up his cross, and follow Me" (Matt. 16:24). So the answer to the question, "What shall I do with Jesus who is called Christ?" is simply this: Believe in Him, receive Him as your Savior, and follow Him the rest of your life.

Put Him *First*

Putting Christ first is going a step further. It is not enough to receive Christ as our Savior and seek to follow Him—we must put Him first in our lives in all matters. Some allow Christ to walk across the threshold of their heart's door, but they do not turn over all the rooms in the house to His charge. In just one or two matters they cling to their own desires and plans. But Jesus asks that we make a complete sacrifice of all our talents, our plans, our possessions, our wills, and our bodies so that in all things He may have the preeminence. This is the key to a victorious and fruitful Christian life.

Jesus is on your hands today. You must come to a decision. Don't try to put Him away, for that is impossible. Don't try to put Him off, for that is dangerous. Don't try to put Him aside, for that is foolish. Put Him on in all His purity and love, and put Him first in every phase of your life.

3

JESUS AND THE
RICH YOUNG RULER

Scripture passage: **Mark 10:17-22**

> Now as He was going out on the road, one came running, knelt before Him, and asked Him, "Good Teacher, what shall I do that I may inherit eternal life?"
>
> So Jesus said to him, "Why do you call Me good? No one is good but One, that is, God. You know the commandments: 'Do not commit adultery,' 'Do not murder,' 'Do not steal,' 'Do not bear false witness,' 'Do not defraud,' 'Honor your father and your mother.'"
>
> And he answered and said to Him, "Teacher, all these things I have observed from my youth."
>
> Then Jesus, looking at him, loved him, and said to him, "One thing you lack: Go your way, sell whatever you have and give to the poor, and you will have treasure in heaven; and come, take up the cross, and follow Me."
>
> But he was sad at this word, and went away grieved, for he had great possessions.

Key verses: "One came running, knelt before Him . . . [He] went away grieved" (vv. 17, 22).

It makes a difference how we answer the question, "What then shall I do with Jesus who is called Christ?" Here we have the account of an individual who came face-to-face with Christ, turned his back on Him, and missed the way to eternal life.

This is one of the great action stories of the New Testament. It has all the elements of a good story: plot, movement, color, contrast, suspense, and climax. It is not fiction, but history—the tragic account of one who stood at the crossroads of life, made the wrong decision, and as far as we know, elected an eternal destiny of darkness. You can't read this story, if you are thoughtful at all, without being depressed in spirit.

When he came to Jesus, this man had a number of good qualities in his favor. He was *earnest*—he came running. He was on important business and didn't have time to spare. He was *humble*—he knelt at the Master's feet. Even though he was rich and a man of status, he knelt in the dust of the road. He was *sincere*—he asked the most important question an individual could ask in life: "What must I do to inherit eternal life?" This was no trivial talk; this was serious. Finally, Matthew's Gospel tells us that he was a *young* man (Matt. 19:20). He was on the threshold of life with all his future before him. But he was thinking about eternal values.

However, we need to look much deeper at the character of this young man in order to understand the tragedy of his final choice. Four statements describe the state of the enquirer. With the Holy Spirit's help, let us think about these:

He was so rich and yet so poor. Verse 22 tells us that the young man "had great possessions." We can probably infer from the way he phrased his question to Jesus—"What shall I do that I may *inherit* eternal life?"—that he had received his estate through inheritance. He probably had houses and land, perhaps a thriving business, and many servants in his household. He likely had fine clothing, good food, and many of the comforts of life. So from the material standpoint he was well off.

However, from the spiritual perspective, the young man was poor. He lacked life's most important possession—eternal life. It is possible for a person to be rich in material goods but at the same time be spiritually bankrupt. The opposite is also true—a person may be poor materially, but rich spiritually.

When I was a missionary in India, I was once conducting revival meetings in a certain city in northwest India. One day I was invited as a guest to the palace of the Maharajah of the state, one of the richest men in the country. He had several Rolls Royce cars in the garage, was dressed in silk clothes, with priceless diamonds, rubies, and emeralds adorning his turban. We ate and drank out of silver vessels. I was amazed at the display of wealth. But at the same time I realized that here was a man who was a spiritual pauper. He had just returned from a trip to Europe and brought back with him a beautiful young night club dancer as his concubine. He had no interest in spiritual matters whatsoever.

The very next day I was invited for tea to a humble Christian home. When I entered the house, the host said to me, "Sir, we have a very humble home; we don't have much in the things of this world, but we offer you the best hospitality that we have. We are so glad to have you in our home." Then he introduced me to his wife, son, and two daughters. I discovered they were all committed Christians, serving the Lord in different ways. After some light refreshments, the host asked me to read a passage of Scripture and then lead in prayer.

When I finished, I said to the father, "My friend, when I entered your home, you said this is a humble home and that you don't have much in material things. But I want to tell you that you are *spiritually* rich. There is so much love, faith, and commitment in this home. You are most fortunate to have such a fine Christian home."

The young man who came to Jesus was rich in body but poor in soul.

He was so good and yet so bad. In response to the young man's question, "What must I do to inherit eternal life?" Jesus quoted the Ten Commandments. The young man replied, "Sir, all of these have I kept from my youth up." He was a moral, upright person who had kept the commandments. Certainly he was an acceptable member of the synagogue, an earnest observer of the moral requirements of that institution.

But at the same time this individual committed the greatest sin possible: he rejected Jesus. This is far more serious than the sin of lying, stealing, killing, or committing adultery. For when a person rejects Christ and the salvation He offers, there is no hope eternally.

Natural goodness is not enough in the sight of God. It is mere painted vice, or like filthy rags in His sight. Sin is heart trouble, not just a skin disease. The young man had a good complexion but an evil heart. He was good according to human standards, but he said no to Jesus.

Furthermore, righteousness is not something negative—it is positive in nature. Notice that all the Ten Commandments but one are negative in character: Thou *shalt not* . . . Thou *shalt not* . . . But Jesus came along and condensed the commandments into two great positive commands. The first four commandments, which have to do with one's relationship to God, He summed up in the first commandment:

"You shall love the LORD your God with all your heart, with all your soul, with all your mind, and with all your strength" (Mark 12:30). The next six commandments, which have to do with one's relationship with his fellow human beings, Jesus summed up in the second great commandment: "You shall love your neighbor as yourself" (v. 31).

Did the young man live up to these two great commandments? Did he love God supremely, above everything else? No! Actually he had an idol in his heart. He loved his possessions more than anything else in the world. He did not love God, or he would have gladly accepted His Son. Did he love his fellow human beings sincerely? No, or he would have gladly bestowed his goods to the poor.

True righteousness is not negative, not simply refraining from doing certain things. It is positive—loving God, accepting His Son, and serving people in need.

The young man who came to Jesus was outwardly good but inwardly evil.

He was so wise and yet so foolish. We can say that the young man was wise, because he asked the most important question anyone could ask: "What must I do to have eternal life?" You can tell something about a person's intelligence by the questions he asks and by his conversation. This was no shallow or frivolous talk that the young man was engaged in with Jesus. He asked a deep, intensely practical question.

Furthermore, the young man did the wisest possible thing with his question. He didn't go to the rabbi or chief priest for an answer—he was seeking life, so he went to the Lord of life himself. Wise people know where to go for the right answers to their questions.

But in spite of all these traits of wisdom, the young man was so foolish in his response. He received the answer to his question—but then made the wrong choice and missed the way. He wanted eternal life but rejected the terms. The most foolish thing a person can do in life is to reject Jesus, who is Life itself.

This individual thought that eternal life was a problem to be solved but found it to be a Person to be received.

A man came to famous evangelist Dwight L. Moody and said to him, "Mr. Moody, if you can tonight furnish me with a satisfactory solution to each of these questions, I'll come back tomorrow night and give my heart to Christ."

Mr. Moody replied, "No, my friend, you're putting it the wrong way. If you'll come to Christ tonight and accept Him as your personal Savior—and then return with your list tomorrow night—I'll answer to your satisfaction every question you have."

The truth is not so much that Christ *gives* the answer to our questions—He *is* the answer.

When Jesus quoted the Ten Commandments to the young man, that was not the real answer to his question. Even if he could have kept all the commandments perfectly, he still would not have found eternal life. Even when Jesus said to him, "Go your way, sell whatever you have and give to the poor," that was not the real answer to the man's question. The real answer was when Jesus said to him, "Come, follow Me." For he who has the Son has life. Eternal life is the result of a personal relationship with Jesus Christ.

He was so near and yet so far. He came close to Jesus, but not in contact with Him. There was geographical proximity, but no spiritual relationship.

Many in history have come close to Jesus, but not close enough. Pilate got close to Jesus—talked to Him, questioned Him, sensed His majesty. But in the end he went so far from Him. Judas got close to Jesus—slept at His side, ate at the same table, traveled with Him, even kissed Him on the cheek. But in the end he went out and hung himself. The young man of this story came close to Jesus—touched His feet, talked to Him, even found a way into His heart, for the record tells us that "Jesus, looking at him, *loved* him." He was so loved, but in the end so *lost*. He asked his question, received the answer, then turned and walked away from Jesus.

He came running—eager and excited. He walked away slowly, sad and lonely. No one can come face-to-face with Jesus and then turn his or her back on Him and go away joyful. This person will walk into darkness and despair.

Many today are so close to Jesus, but in their hearts so far from Him. They are members of the church, have been baptized in His name, know all about Him and His teachings but still have not made personal contact with Him. They have never taken the final step of surrendering their lives to Christ and entering into a personal relationship with Him. They are on the doorstep of the Kingdom—but have never entered in.

The greatest tragedy in life is to come face-to-face with Jesus and then turn your back on Him.

4

JESUS AND THE SAMARITAN WOMAN

Scripture passage: John 4:5-30, 39-42

[Jesus] came to a city of Samaria which is called Sychar, near the plot of ground that Jacob gave to his son Joseph. Now Jacob's well was there. Jesus therefore, being wearied from His journey, sat thus by the well. It was about the sixth hour.

A woman of Samaria came to draw water. Jesus said to her, "Give Me a drink." For His disciples had gone away into the city to buy food.

Then the woman of Samaria said to Him, "How is it that You, being a Jew, ask a drink from me, a Samaritan woman?" For Jews have no dealings with Samaritans.

Jesus answered and said to her, "If you knew the gift of God, and who it is who says to you, 'Give Me a drink,' you would have asked Him, and He would have given you living water."

The woman said to Him, "Sir, You have nothing to draw with, and the well is deep. Where then do You get that living water? Are You greater than our father Jacob, who gave us the well, and drank from it himself, as well as his sons and his livestock?"

Jesus answered and said to her, "Whoever drinks of this water will thirst again, but whoever drinks of the water that I shall give him will never thirst. But the water that I shall give him will become in him a fountain of water springing up into everlasting life."

The woman said to Him, "Sir, give me this water, that I may not thirst, nor come here to draw."

Jesus said to her, "Go, call your husband, and come here."

The woman answered and said, "I have no husband."

Jesus said to her, "You have well said, 'I have no husband,' for you have had five husbands, and the one whom you now have is not your husband; in that you spoke truly."

The woman said to Him, "Sir, I perceive that You are a prophet. Our fathers worshiped on this mountain, and you

Jews say that in Jerusalem is the place where one ought to worship."

Jesus said to her, "Woman, believe Me, the hour is coming when you will neither on this mountain, nor in Jerusalem, worship the Father. You worship what you do not know; we know what we worship, for salvation is of the Jews. But the hour is coming, and now is, when the true worshipers will worship the Father in spirit and truth; for the Father is seeking such to worship Him. God is Spirit, and those who worship Him must worship in spirit and truth."

The woman said to Him, "I know that Messiah is coming" (who is called Christ). "When He comes, He will tell us all things."

Jesus said to her, "I who speak to you am He."

And at this point His disciples came, and they marveled that He talked with a woman; yet no one said, "What do You seek?" or, "Why are You talking with her?"

The woman then left her waterpot, went her way into the city, and said to the men, "Come, see a Man who told me all things that I ever did. Could this be the Christ?" Then they went out of the city and came to Him. . . .

And many of the Samaritans of that city believed in Him because of the word of the woman who testified, "He told me all that I ever did." So when the Samaritans had come to Him, they urged Him to stay with them; and He stayed there two days. And many more believed because of His own word.

Then they said to the woman, "Now we believe, not because of what you said, for we have heard for ourselves and know that this is indeed the Christ, the Savior of the world."

Key verse: "Come, see a Man who told me all things that I ever did. Could this be the Christ?" (v. 29).

The story of the rich young ruler illustrates the tragedy of being confronted by Christ and then rejecting His claims. The story of the woman at the well of Sychar demonstrates the marvelous transformation that takes place when an individual responds in faith to Christ.

Let us note carefully the method that Jesus used in confronting the woman, and the progressive faith response that she made.

Jesus sought her soul. Jesus was on His way to Galilee when He came to a city in Samaria called Sychar. Just outside the city was Jacob's well. Being weary from the journey, Jesus sat down on the parapet of the well, and along came a woman with her waterpot to draw water for her household needs. It is significant that she came all alone and at midday, contrary to the custom of women in the Middle East. She probably came at this odd hour because she was a woman of ill repute in the city and wanted to avoid the contemptuous gaze and scornful remarks of the other women. As she came closer to the well, she saw a man sitting there. To her He was just a man, a Jew, a stranger, nothing more.

But Jesus saw more than just a woman. He saw a person with spiritual needs, a potential child of God. So He sought her soul. This was the only thing she had of any value. With her virtue gone, her character marred, her reputation soiled, and her body given over to lust, she was ready for the junk pile of the universe. But Jesus looked beyond all this and saw something of eternal value in this sinful woman. She had a soul that needed to be saved, a life that needed to be rescued. Once delivered from her wretched past, she could become a mighty power for God and good. So when Jesus sat down upon the side of the well on that hot, dusty day many centuries ago, He was interested not merely in making conversation, He was interested not merely in quenching His thirst—He was in quest of a soul, a life. This was big business.

Jesus secured her interest. *By referring to something she knew.* Jesus met the woman on common ground. She needed water, and so did He. So He asked a favor—"Give Me a drink." Jesus wanted to lead from the known to the unknown. The woman knew about the water in the well, but she did not know of the water of eternal life. She knew of the well of Sychar but not of Christ, the fountain of spiritual satisfaction. She knew about Jacob, but she did not know the Messiah. Jesus was getting down to her level of understanding.

By offering something she needed. In response to Jesus' request, the woman said, "How is it You, being a Jew, ask a drink from me, a Samaritan woman?" to which Jesus replied, "If you knew the gift of God, and who it is who says to you, 'Give Me a drink,' you would have asked Him, and He would have given you living water. . . . Whoever drinks of this water will thirst again, but whoever drinks of the water that I shall give him will never thirst. But the water that I shall give him will become in him a fountain of water springing up into everlasting life."

Immediately the woman's interest was secured, her curiosity aroused, her desire quickened. What was this living water? Who was this stranger? She wanted to know more, to get this something she did not have. Now she saw in Jesus more than just an ordinary man. He was a special person, greater even than the patriarch Jacob. So she said to Jesus, "Sir, give me this water."

Jesus shocked her conscience. After Jesus had aroused the woman's interest and spiritual desire, He now went straight to the sore point in her life. She wanted the living water, yes; she longed for something better, true. But she would have to settle the sin question first; she would have to set right the past. So Jesus tactfully asked her to go call her husband. The woman replied, "I have no husband."

Jesus responded, "You have well said, 'I have no husband,' for you have had five husbands, and the one whom you now have is not your husband; in that you spoke truly."

Astonished, the woman blurted out, "Sir, I perceive that You are a prophet."

Her conscience was smitten. Her sin came before her eyes. She had to face the question squarely; there was no sidetracking the issue. Jesus never treated sin lightly; to Him it was a moral tragedy. He loved the sinner, but He hated sin. If the Samaritan woman wanted the living water, there was only one way. She must repent of her sin and forsake her evil life.

The Samaritan woman now brought up a theological point: "Our fathers worshiped on this mountain, and you Jews say that in Jerusalem is the place where one ought to worship."

Jesus replied in essence that it's not where but *how* one worships that's important, for God is Spirit, and those who worship Him must worship in spirit and truth.

The woman said to Jesus, "I know the Messiah is coming (who is called Christ). When He comes, He will tell us all things."

Then Jesus said to her, "I who speak to you am He."

The eyes of the woman were now opened. The stranger was no longer just an important man. He was more than just a prophet. He was the Messiah, the Christ. She knew it in her mind; she believed it in her heart.

Jesus satisfied her heart. The Samaritan woman was excited. She forgot the well and her waterpot and with joy ran to tell about Jesus. She said to everyone, "Come, see a Man who told me all things that I ever did. Could this be the Christ?" So convincing was her testimony and so remarkable the change in her attitude, that the whole town came out to see this Stranger of Galilee. She had found the water of life; her heart had been satisfied, her life changed. She who had once led men astray now led them to the feet of the Savior. The interesting thing is that the disciples also went into town, but what did they bring back with them? Bread and fish—that's all. They met several people in town, but they never said to anyone, "The Messiah is sitting at Jacob's well—would you like to come and meet Him?" They returned with their groceries, but no one was with them. The woman, on the other hand, went into town, gave her witness, and brought a multitude of people back with her. The result was a spiritual revival that swept through the whole town.

When a person meets Christ and discovers that He is the Messiah, the Savior of the world, he or she will never be the same!

5

JESUS—IMMANUEL: THE INCARNATION

Four major events characterize the Person of Jesus Christ—His incarnation, His crucifixion, His resurrection, and His second coming. The next four chapters center on these events.

Scripture passage: **Luke 19:1-10**

Jesus entered and passed through Jericho. Now behold, there was a man named Zacchaeus who was a chief tax collector, and he was rich. And he sought to see who Jesus was, but could not because of the crowd, for he was of short stature. So he ran ahead and climbed up into a sycamore tree to see Him, for He was going to pass that way.

And when Jesus came to the place, He looked up and saw him, and said to him, "Zacchaeus, make haste and come down, for today I must stay at your house." So he made haste and came down, and received Him joyfully.

But when they saw it, they all murmured, saying, "He has gone to be a guest with a man who is a sinner."

Then Zacchaeus stood and said to the Lord, "Look, Lord, I give half of my goods to the poor; and if I have taken anything from anyone by false accusation, I restore fourfold."

And Jesus said to him, "Today salvation has come to this house, because he also is a son of Abraham; for the Son of Man has come to seek and to save that which was lost."

Key verse: "For the Son of Man has come to seek and to save that which was lost" (v. 10).

The greatest event in history is not human beings going to the moon but God coming to earth. This is the divine invasion of the human race, in which God in the person of Jesus came into this world and into history from the outside. "[He] made Himself of no reputation, taking the form of a servant, and coming in the likeness of men" (Phil. 2:7).

The Son of Man has come! Yes, but why? Why did He come to that remote little village atop the Judaean hills, come by motherhood's painful labor, in a manger among the cattle, by starlight while shepherds guarded their sheep? Why did He come to the poverty of a simple peasant home, to a woman's heart of love and to a king's heart of hate, to a world so lacking in hospitality as to afford Him only a borrowed cradle at His birth and a borrowed tomb at His death? You may be sure there was a reason, and a mighty reason at that—for divine movements such as we have in Jesus are never without purpose. The reason may be beyond our human comprehension, but it is always there nonetheless.

Looking now at the text, note that it naturally divides itself into three major points: (1) The personality of the Son of Man, (2) the plight of humanity, and (3) the purpose of Christ's coming.

The Personality of the Savior

He bears a unique title—the "Son of Man." Notice, the verse does not say "*a* son of man" but "*the* Son of Man." It is a title that the Master chose himself. It occurs 32 times in Matthew, 15 times in Mark, 26 times in Luke, 12 times in John—85 times in all, and only twice used by anyone but the Master himself. It is a term that speaks specifically of His real union and identification with humanity. He was more than the Son of Abraham, more than the Son of David, more than the Son of Mary. He has no racial, tribal, or family limitations. He is "the Son of Man." He is the universal One. He is man's true Man—perfect Man! Very real to Him were the human experiences through which He passed. He experienced our poverty, felt our pain, suffered our hunger, tasted our sorrows, met our temptations, and sank into our death. And because of this sharing in the actual experiences of humanity, Jesus has become our merciful and faithful High Priest. How full and rich are His sympathies!

But any attempt to explain Christ as a mere man is certainly missing the mark. The humanity of His personality was no more real than

His divinity. As a man He became hungry and asked for bread, but as God He declared, "I am the bread of life." As a man He was thirsty and asked for a drink, but as God He offered the living water that can quench all thirst. As a man He walked on the dusty roads of Palestine, but as God He walked on the waters of the Sea of Galilee. As a man He was crucified on a cross and His body laid in a tomb, but as God He arose from the dead and announced, "I am the resurrection and the life" (John 11:25). He was God "manifest in the flesh," and in Him "God was . . . reconciling the world to Himself" (2 Cor. 5:19).

The Plight of Humanity

Humanity's plight is revealed in one powerful, tragic word: *lost.* "The Son of Man has come to seek and to save that which was lost" (Luke 19:10). Broadly speaking, the Scriptures locate the motives that lay back of the coming of Christ into two great facts: the love of God and the need of humanity. Guilt on one side, and grace on the other. Divine pity meeting the human plight.

Lost! It is a word that stabs like a knife. Is it a purse containing our financial savings? Is it a pet that has strayed away from the friendly compound? Is it a child who has been swallowed up in the milling throng of a shopping mall? Is it a traveler who has lost his way in the forest? Is it a ship off its course, being pounded to pieces on the rocks? No, not that, but something infinitely greater and vastly more tragic! It is a world of lost men and women—lost from God and therefore groping in darkness, lost from life and therefore eking out a purposeless existence, lost from peace and therefore torn by strife and dissatisfaction.

Lost! Not simply the Jew, but the Gentile as well. Not merely the limited world of Christ's day, but the entire world of our advanced day. The vision of the Son of Man is all-inclusive. It takes in all people, whether lost in suburban mansion or inner-city ghetto, in university classroom or prison cell, in sprawling metropolis or secluded village. "All we like sheep have gone astray; we have turned, every one, to his own way," declares the prophet Isaiah (53:6).

In a day when sin is smiled upon, when human pride denies the very disease that is undermining civilization, when evil is flaunted in the face of the public, it is time to act. It is time for ten thousand pulpits to cry into the ears and consciences of people the sober, solemn, stubborn fact that apart from Christ, apart from personal surrender to

Him and saving faith in Him, they are lost and they shall die in their sins. This is the plight that moved the Son of God to become the Son of Man and sent Him shamefully to the Cross.

The Purpose of the Savior

Why did Jesus come to earth? The answer is not hard to find. Listen: "The Son of Man has come to seek and to save that which was lost." Here we have it stated briefly and simply—*to seek and to save.* Not to be a great teacher, writing books and founding schools, not to establish a new system of philosophy or a new religion, not to establish a new social order or a new political empire—but "to seek and to save that which was lost." His mission was purely redemptive.

In each of the four Gospels we have from the lips of the Master himself at least one clear-cut statement concerning the purpose of His ministry, and in each instance it is His work as Redeemer that is emphasized.

Matthew records these words of Jesus: "I did not come to call the righteous, but sinners, to repentance" (9:13). Mark records, "For even the Son of Man did not come to be served, but to serve, and to give His life a ransom for many" (10:45). John records, "God did not send His Son into the world to condemn the world, but that the world through Him might be saved" (3:17). Then add to that the statement from Luke's Gospel: "The Son of Man has come to seek and to save that which was lost."

In many parts of the world we hear people say that they are earnestly seeking God—through meditation and study, through worship and ritual, through pilgrimages and sacrifices. What a revolution in our thinking our text produces! We don't need to seek God—*He* is seeking *us!* In this matter of redemption, He is the Prime Mover. It was so in the Garden of Eden. The divine question "Adam, where are you?" is framed in the picture in which we see humanity in hiding and God on the quest. It has been thus down through the ages. Jesus, the Good Shepherd, has been out on the mountaintop, searching for the lost sheep.

Jesus came to seek and to save the lost—the lost down-and-outer in the slum, the lost social gadabout in the mansion, the lost prodigal in night club carousing, the lost Magdalene in failure and shame. He's seeking the lost university student in atheism or religious indifference, the lost church member, the moralist, the Pharisee, the Nicodemus—the lost anybody, the lost everybody, the lost you, the lost me.

Christ has sought and found and renewed all who have opened their hearts to Him. Will you open your heart today? Open it in confession of your sins. Open it in personal, simple acceptance of Christ as your own Savior. If you will do this, then the meaning of His coming to earth will be realized not only *by* you but *in* you and *through* you.

Remember: the Son of God became the Son of Man in order that the children of men and women might become the children of God.

6

JESUS—SAVIOR: THE CRUCIFIXION

Scripture passage: Luke 23:33-37, 39-43

When they had come to the place called Calvary, there they crucified Him, and the criminals, one on the right hand and the other on the left. Then Jesus said, "Father, forgive them, for they do not know what they do." And they divided His garments and cast lots.

And the people stood looking on. But even the rulers with them sneered, saying, "He saved others; let Him save Himself if He is the Christ, the chosen of God."

And the soldiers also mocked Him, coming and offering Him sour wine, and saying, "If You are the King of the Jews, save Yourself." . . .

Then one of the criminals who were hanged blasphemed Him, saying, "If You are the Christ, save Yourself and us."

But the other, answering, rebuked him, saying, "Do you not even fear God, seeing you are under the same condemnation? And we indeed justly, for we receive the due reward of our deeds; but this Man has done nothing wrong."

Then he said to Jesus, "Lord, remember me when You come into Your kingdom."

And Jesus said to him, "Assuredly, I say to you, today you will be with Me in Paradise."

Key verses: "And He, bearing His cross, went out to a place called the Place of a Skull, which is called in Hebrew, Golgotha, where they crucified Him, and two others with Him, one on either side, and Jesus in the center" (John 19:17-18).

We usually speak of just one cross, but we must not forget that there were three crosses, that three men died on that fateful day in history. It was not mere accident that Jesus died between two thieves. Even this detail of the Crucifixion was in accordance with the eternal plan of God. Hereby God was trying to teach humanity some eternal facts and was seeking to reveal certain basic truths of the plan of salvation.

There were three crosses and three men who died. But what a tremendous difference in the death of these three! Christ died *for* sin. One thief died *to* sin. The other died *in* sin. Christ died as the *Savior of sinners*. One thief died as a *saved sinner;* and the other died as a *condemned sinner.*

The Cross of Redemption—Christ Died for Sin

What a mighty difference there was between Christ and the two men who died by His side! He was *innocent* and *sinless;* they were *guilty* and *sinful.* All gave testimony to the sinlessness of Christ. The Roman governor Pilate, who conducted the trial, said, "I find no fault in Him at all" (John 18:38). Pilate's wife, who suffered a disturbing dream concerning Christ, sent word to her husband: "Have nothing to do with that just Man" (Matt. 27:19). Judas, who betrayed Him, cried out, "I have sinned by betraying innocent blood" (v. 4). One of the men who died by His side said to his companion, "This Man has done nothing wrong" (Luke 23:41). Peter, who walked close by His side for three whole years, testified, "[He] committed no sin, nor was guile found in His mouth" (1 Pet. 2:22). Friend and foe alike testified to the spotless purity of the Master.

The two men who died by His side stood out in dire contrast. Matthew and Mark both state that they were "robbers" (Matt. 27:38; Mark 15:27). Luke refers to them as "criminals" (23:32). One of the men himself confessed, "We indeed [suffer] justly, for we receive the due reward of our deeds" (Luke 23:41).

There was another significant difference. Jesus was *divine;* but the two thieves were *human.* As mortal beings, they were subject to death; sooner or later they must die. It's true—they were dying as criminals before their time—but even so, they must die sometime. As for Christ, being God, He was not subject to death. He has no beginning or end; birth and death have no control over Him. But herein lies the marvel of the Incarnation and the Crucifixion. God, who never dies and cannot die, actually took upon himself the form of a man for the express purpose of dying.

"Christ Jesus . . . being in the form of God, did not consider it robbery to be equal with God, but made Himself of no reputation, taking the form of a servant, and coming in the likeness of men. And being found in appearance as a man, He humbled Himself and became obedient to the point of death, even the death of the cross" (Phil. 2:5-8).

What a staggering thought! Jesus didn't have to die, but He chose to die in our place.

That middle cross did not belong to Jesus; it belonged to another, Barabbas. And who was Barabbas? An insurrectionist, a thief, a murderer (see Luke 23:25; John 18:40). He was a greater sinner and deserved more to die than Jesus' two companions on Calvary. But in urging Pilate as to whom he should release, the mob cried, "Not this Man, but Barabbas!" And so Barabbas went free while Christ went to the Cross. He took Barabbas's place. But more than that, He took the place of every human being who has ever lived or ever will live, for in reality that middle cross was your cross and my cross. We deserved to die, but Christ died for us. He took upon himself our sins, our punishment, our shame, our death. And so God died for humanity, the innocent for the guilty, the sinless for the sinful, the eternal for the mortal. There was no other way out. The Cross was an absolute necessity for the salvation of the world.

Jesus died on the middle cross as the Savior of sinners.

The Cross of Repentance—One Thief Died to Sin

At first he, too, joined in with the people and his companion in reviling the Savior: "If You are the Christ, save Yourself and us" (Luke 23:39). Both Matthew and Mark state very clearly that both men reviled Him (Matt. 27:44; Mark 15:32). But then something happened in the mind of the one thief. He closely watched the Savior and listened to every word He spoke. He noticed that in spite of the jeering and cursing of the angry mob, the Master never once opened His mouth to rebuke or curse. In patience He bore it all. The thief also noticed that Jesus thought not of himself but of His mother and her welfare. Then he heard the Master call out, "Father, forgive them; for they know not what they do" (Luke 23:34, KJV). This was too much for the man at His side. His heart was broken. He saw his own sin and the sinlessness of the Man on the middle cross. He realized that this was more than man—yes, a prophet; indeed, the Christ. And so he repented.

He confessed his sin. "We receive the due reward of our deeds"

(v. 41), he said to the other thief. He recognized his guilt.

He turned to the Savior for mercy. "Lord, remember me when You come into Your kingdom" (v. 42), he cried.

And the Savior, in spite of His agony and personal distress, turned to him in love and said, "Today you will be with Me in Paradise" (v. 43). Oh, the depth of His love, the marvel of His grace, the greatness of His salvation! "Today"—a present-tense salvation. "You will be with Me"—a perfect salvation. "In Paradise"—a permanent salvation.

And so the first thief died to sin and died a sinner saved by grace. That cross stands for the eternal truth that no matter how deep we have fallen into sin, no matter when we turn to Him in repentance, God will always stand ready and willing to forgive and redeem. If there was hope for that wretched thief on the cross, there is hope for you and me.

The Cross of Retribution—the Second Thief Died in His Sins

From the beginning right up to the last moment, the second thief railed upon the Savior with cursing and blasphemy. Like his companion, he, too, saw the patience and love and forgiving spirit of the Man dying in the middle. He, too, must have been convicted of his own guilt and sin. The contrast between Christ and himself was too great for him not to realize his condition. Like his companion, he, too, had the opportunity to repent and turn to the Savior for forgiveness and eternal life. But instead, he hardened his heart, refused to repent, and so died in his sins, unsaved, without hope.

What a tragedy of tragedies! Just think of it—he, too, could have that very day gone to be with the Lord forever, but instead he went from the presence of the Lord for all eternity. The Son of God was dying for the sins of the world, was dying even for *his* sins, at his very side, but the unrepentant thief died without ever knowing the joy of forgiveness or the power of God's grace.

That third cross stands forever as a solemn warning to all humanity. Christ's death is *efficacious* for the sins of the whole world, but it is *effective* only to those who repent and believe. If we believe, our sins are taken away, washed, covered by the blood, buried in the depths of the sea, separated from us as far as the east is from the west. But if we refuse to believe, our sins will remain upon us and separate us from the Lord forever.

Many look at the second cross without looking at the third. They say, "What's the hurry? There's plenty of time. Let me have my fling now. At the last moment I can repent and be saved." But they forget that the man on the third cross did not repent, did not believe, and so died in his sins. If such people take comfort from the second cross, they should also take warning from the third cross. And as for the thief who repented, that was his first and last opportunity to repent and believe.

But as for us, we have had countless opportunities. We have heard innumerable sermons, and if we keep on neglecting God's grace and mercy, there will come a time when the Spirit of God will cease to strive with us. Then when death approaches, we will not be able to repent.

For no one can repent just whenever he or she likes. Even repentance is not of ourselves; it is the gift of God. The time to repent is when the Spirit of God reveals our sins and gives us the grace to repent. Furthermore, there is no guarantee that we will suffer a slow and lingering death, like the thief on the cross, that will give us time for thought and repentance. Death may strike suddenly and swiftly, giving us no time to turn to God.

All humanity is thus divided into two camps. The middle cross has drawn a line down through the whole of humanity. On one side stands the repentant, the believing, the redeemed. On the other side stands the unrepentant, the unbelieving, the condemned. The one group has died *to* sin; the other group will die *in* sin. On which side of the Cross are you?

Your sin is in one of two places today. It is either on the Savior, or it is on you. If you repent and believe, your sin will be rolled from you on to Him; if you neglect and refuse, your sin will remain upon you. It all depends on how you look at the middle cross, the cross of the Savior.

7

JESUS—VICTOR: THE RESURRECTION

Scripture passage: Matt. 28:1-10

Now after the Sabbath, as the first day of the week began to dawn, Mary Magdalene and the other Mary came to see the tomb.

And behold, there was a great earthquake; for an angel of the Lord descended from heaven, and came and rolled back the stone from the door, and sat on it. His countenance was like lightning, and his clothing as white as snow. And the guards shook for fear of him, and became like dead men.

But the angel answered and said to the women, "Do not be afraid, for I know that you seek Jesus who was crucified. He is not here; for He is risen, as He said. Come, see the place where the Lord lay. And go quickly and tell His disciples that He is risen from the dead, and indeed He is going before you into Galilee; there you will see Him. Behold, I have told you."

So they departed quickly from the tomb with fear and great joy, and ran to bring His disciples word. And as they went to tell His disciples, behold, Jesus met them, saying, "Rejoice!" And they came and held Him by the feet and worshiped Him. Then Jesus said to them, "Do not be afraid. Go and tell My brethren to go to Galilee, and there they will see Me."

Key verse: "He is not here; for He is risen, as He said" (v. 6).

The resurrection of our Lord Jesus Christ is the bedrock of Christian evidences and the collapse of infidelity. For this reason Gulam Ahmed, founder of the Ahmediyya sect of Islam, said to his disciples at the end of his life, "If you want to strike a deathblow at Christianity, strike directly at the Resurrection. Destroy the Christian's faith in the resurrection of Christ, and he will have nothing left. Convince the Christian that Christ never arose from the dead, and the battle will be ours."

He was right. The Christian faith either stands or falls with the resurrection of our Lord.

The Resurrection is intrinsic to the longings of every human heart. Something within us cries out for it; faith demands it.

The apostle Paul wrote in his letter to the Corinthian church that if there is no Resurrection, then "we are of all men the most pitiable" (1 Cor. 15:19); "our preaching is vain and your faith is also vain" (v. 14); "you are still in your sins" (v. 17). If there is no Resurrection, then the grave is the end; we have no message, no foundation for faith, no salvation, no hope.

But the moment you introduce the truth of the Resurrection, then our message becomes a living force, our faith takes hold, salvation becomes a glorious possibility, and our hope for the future becomes bright.

The resurrection of Christ was very real to the early disciples. It transformed their lives. It turned them from fearful, vacillating disciples into courageous, mighty apostles. The resurrection of Christ (along with the death of Christ) was the central theme of their preaching. This truth brought into being the Christian Church.

Now let us look at the Resurrection account as found in the scripture passage above. We'll think about this thrilling story under a threefold heading: (1) The Vanquished Stone; (2) The Vacant Sepulchre; and (3) The Victorious Savior.

The Vanquished Stone

At the suggestion of the Jewish religious leaders, Pilate commanded the tomb of Christ be sealed with a huge stone and that a guard be placed on watch. The Jews, remembering the words of Christ, were fearful that the disciples would come in the night, steal the body of Christ, and then spread the news that He had risen from the dead. Thus their deep concern over the tomb.

We see in these precautions a concerted attempt on the part of the forces of evil to keep Christ from rising from the dead. The last thing they desired was that Christ should emerge from the tomb. Their victory now seemed complete—the matchless life, the challenging words, the miraculous deeds of the Master were forever stilled. The little band of followers was dispersed. Hopes of the common people were dashed to the ground. So the enemies of Christ sealed the tomb; the Roman officials tried to make it secure. All hell rejoiced.

But all of Satan's forces put together were no match for one solitary angel. "Behold . . . an angel of the Lord descended from heaven, and came and rolled back the stone from the door, and sat on it." Do you get the picture? The angel *sat on the stone!* As if to say, no stone, no guard, no government can hold back the Lord of life! It was a symbol of Christ's absolute triumph over death, hell, and the grave. The stone that had sealed the tomb now became the seat for an angel from heaven!

The Vacant Sepulchre

When the women came weeping to the tomb early at dawn, the angel said to them, "Why do you seek the living among the dead? He is not here, but is risen!" (Luke 24:5-6). Those who entered the tomb found no body. Jesus' linen clothes were folded neatly and laid to one side. The tomb was empty! In fact, it was empty even before the angel rolled away the stone. For the angel did not roll away the stone so that Jesus could come out—he rolled it away so the women could go in and see that the tomb was empty.

An Indian evangelist was preaching in the open air one day when a Muslim suddenly interrupted him by saying, "Wait a minute, sir. We Muslims have something that you Christians do not have."

"What is it?" asked the preacher.

"I'll tell you," replied the Muslim. "We Muslims can go to Medina in Arabia and stand at the tomb of our prophet Mohammed and say, 'Here lies the body of our prophet Mohammed.' You Christians have no tomb at which to worship."

With a smile the evangelist replied, "Thank God—we Christians have no tomb because we have *no corpse!*"

We do not worship a dead body, but a living Christ. Graves of human beings are respected for their *occupancy*. We stand at the grave of a loved one or friend and say to ourselves, "Here lies the body of my wife [husband, son, daughter, mother, father, friend]." But Christ's tomb is revered for its *vacancy*. He is *not* in the tomb. He is alive forevermore!

The Victorious Savior

"He is not here; for He is risen," declared the angel. He is risen not merely in spirit, not merely as a ghost, but risen in real flesh and blood. It is no wonder that Paul cries out in triumph, "O Death, where is your sting? O Hades, where is your victory?" (1 Cor. 15:55). For in His resurrection, Christ triumphed once and for all over death, hell, and the grave. And now He can declare to the whole world, "I am the resurrection and the life . . . whoever lives and believes in Me shall never die" (John 11:25-26).

In the Resurrection the forces of evil were completely routed. Satan was dealt a fatal blow, and death was robbed of its sting. Now we no longer fear death. For death has become the door leading into the blessed life of heaven—yes, leading into the very presence of God. Death is merely God's anesthesia while He is changing our bodies. And when we stand at the grave of a loved one or friend, we realize that this is not final. We have been separated merely for a season, and there is glorious reunion ahead.

An aged caretaker of Winchester Cathedral in southern England loved to tell the story of how the news of Wellington's victory over Napoleon reached England. News of the history-making battle came by a sailing vessel to the south coast of England and then was signaled by flags (semaphore) to London. Eagerly the empire waited for news from the battlefront. Atop the cathedral the semaphore began slowly to spell out the message, letter by letter: W-e-l-l-i-n-g-t-o-n d-e-f-e-a-t-e-d. On those who thought this was the end of the message, a dark gloom suddenly descended. But there was more: t-h-e e-n-e-m-y. This news spread like prairie fire over the land, lifting the people from gloom to gladness and praise.

To the disciples on Friday, the Cross meant one thing—Jesus defeated. But suddenly on Easter morning the fog lifted, and the glorious radiance of the first Lord's Day morning flooded Joseph's tomb, announcing the joyful, gloom-dispelling news: *Jesus defeated the enemy.*

"He is not here!" shouted the angel. Therefore, He is *everywhere!* Because He is not in the tomb, He is with me in the office, in the school, in the factory, in the home, in the marketplace. He is with me wherever I go. "Lo, I am with you always, even to the end of the age" (Matt. 28:20).

8

JESUS—COMING KING: THE SECOND COMING

Scripture passage: Acts 1:4-12

And being assembled together with them, He commanded them not to depart from Jerusalem, but to wait for the
Promise of the Father, "which," He said, "you have heard
from Me; for John truly baptized with water, but you shall be
baptized with the Holy Spirit not many days from now."

Therefore, when they had come together, they asked
Him, saying, "Lord, will You at this time restore the kingdom
to Israel?"

And He said to them, "It is not for you to know times or
seasons which the Father has put in His own authority. But
you shall receive power when the Holy Spirit has come upon
you; and you shall be witnesses to Me in Jerusalem, and in all
Judea and Samaria, and to the end of the earth."

Now when He had spoken these things, while they
watched, He was taken up, and a cloud received Him out of
their sight.

And while they looked steadfastly toward heaven as He
went up, behold, two men stood by them in white apparel,
who also said, "Men of Galilee, why do you stand gazing up into heaven? This same Jesus, who was taken up from you into
heaven, will so come in like manner as you saw Him go into
heaven."

Then they returned to Jerusalem from the Mount called
Olivet, which is near Jerusalem, a Sabbath day's journey.

Key verse: "This same Jesus, who was taken up from you
into heaven, will so come in like manner as you saw
Him go into heaven" (v. 11).

What is the most certain event in life? Death, you may say. Yes, death is truly a most certain event for all of us—great and small, rich and poor, high and low. "It is appointed for men to die once" (Heb. 9:27). No one can escape the hand of death. Yet there is an event more certain than death, and that is the return of our Lord Jesus Christ. For there will be at least one generation that will not taste death. It is quite possible that He may come in our lifetime, so that we will not experience death. Thus, the fact of our death is not 100 percent certain, but the fact of Christ's return to earth is 100 percent sure.

The Christian looks in two directions. He looks *backward* to the first coming of Christ—to the Cross—in *gratitude*. He looks *forward* to the second coming of Christ—the culmination of His kingdom—in *hope*.

To the Christian the fact of Christ's return is an incentive in his or her spiritual life. It is an incentive to *hope*, for he or she knows that the prince of this world is judged and that righteousness will one day cover the earth as the waters cover the sea. It is an incentive for *purity*, for the Christian knows that without holiness no one will see the Lord (Heb. 12:14). Therefore, "everyone who has this hope in Him purifies himself, just as He is pure" (1 John 3:3). It is an incentive to *service*, for the Christian knows that "the night is coming when no one can work" (John 9:4). He or she knows the time is short and that there is still much to be done.

In attempting to understand the truth of the Second Coming, we have to be careful that we stick to the basic facts and avoid vain theories and imaginations. Much of the teaching concerning the end of time is couched in figurative language that is most difficult to understand (particularly the Book of Revelation). Some of the details we will probably never understand in this life, so it is impossible to be dogmatic about each little item connected with the Second Coming. As to the basic facts of this event, the Scriptures are quite clear, and concerning these we need entertain no doubts. We are safe as long as we stand on the facts.

What are the basic facts of the return of our Lord?

Christ is certainly coming again. It will be a personal appearance, for the angels said to the disciples, "This same Jesus . . . will so come in like manner as you have seen Him go into heaven." It will not be merely a spiritual coming, as is the coming of Christ into the heart of the sinner when he or she believes, or the coming of the Holy Spirit on the Day of Pentecost. Christ himself shall appear, and we shall see Him.

The miracle of television helps us understand the possibility of such an event. One day recently it was announced that the president of the United States would address the nation on an important subject at 9 P.M. At the announced time we turned on the television set in our room, and immediately President Bill Clinton stepped into the room from where the event was being transmitted. We heard every word; we saw every action. And at that very moment he was seen and heard by millions and millions of other people across the entire country. Now if it is possible for the leader of a nation to be seen and heard by everyone throughout the country, I am sure it will be possible for the King of Kings, when He returns, to be seen and heard by all humanity. Just how it will happen we cannot say, but we certainly know it *will* happen.

The time of His return is uncertain. The Bible says that "the day of the Lord so comes as a thief in the night" (1 Thess. 5:2). Jesus himself said, "Of that day and hour no one knows, no, not even the angels of heaven, but My Father only. . . . Therefore you also be ready, for the Son of Man is coming at an hour when you do not expect Him" (Matt. 24:36, 44).

Two dangers should be avoided in this connection. The first is that of setting the time near at hand and therefore refusing to make any long-range plans for the Church and the Kingdom. Those who take this attitude say something like this: "Jesus is coming soon, so don't worry about building churches and starting new projects; just save as many people as you can, as quickly as you can, and be satisfied with that."

The second danger is that of putting the time of the return so far into the future that it loses all significance and incentive for the present. Those who take this attitude argue like this: "Ever since the ascension of the Lord, people have been saying that His return is close at hand, and they've all been wrong. So why worry or get excited about it now? When the time comes, it will come, and that's that."

It appears that the best working philosophy that would avoid both of these dangers is as follows: Live each moment as if He were coming today; work as if He were coming a thousand years from now. This means we will go ahead with all our plans for the future with care and foresight, but at the same time we will be looking and longing for His return every day and will be ready to meet Him whenever He comes.

His coming will be a day of joy to some and a day of sorrow to others. To those who love and serve Him, it will be a day of joy; to those who reject His call and claim, it will be a day of tremendous sorrow. His coming will cause division upon the earth. Jesus said, "Two men will be in the field: one will be taken and the other left. Two women will be grinding at the mill: one will be taken and the other left" (Matt. 24:40-41). Some will be ready to meet Him; others will not.

To those who died in the Lord and to those who now live for Him, the day of Christ's return will be a time of resurrection, reunion, and reward. As Paul writes in 1 Thess. 4:16-17, "The Lord Himself will descend from heaven with a shout, with the voice of an archangel, and with the trumpet of God. And the dead in Christ will rise first. Then we who are alive and remain shall be caught up together with them in the clouds to meet the Lord in the air. And thus we shall always be with the Lord." What a day of rejoicing that will be—to be home with the Lord!

When I was a missionary in India, I was returning from a long and strenuous preaching mission. On the same train a rajah (king of a small state) was returning from a successful tiger hunt. When the train pulled into the station, no one was there to meet me (my wife was up in the hills with the children). But a special guard of honor stood at attention, friends brought beautiful flower garlands, and a band played stirring music to welcome the rajah back home.

I felt sorry for myself and thought, *Is this fair? Here I have been laboring for weeks to proclaim the gospel and bring souls into the kingdom of God, but when I return there is no one to welcome me or give me a word of thanks. As for this rajah, he did nothing more than go on a tiger hunt, and when he returns, bands play and friends shower him with garlands.*

Then I heard an inner voice say, *My son, remember: you are not home yet.*

Let you who toil and suffer for the Master amid misunderstanding and ingratitude and sorrow remember this comforting fact: You are not home yet. But a day is coming when the Lord will reward His children, when He will wipe away all tears, when He will grant them a crown of life.

To those who refuse or neglect the great salvation that is offered in Christ, the day of His return will be a time of judgment and sorrow. John pictures this final tragedy in the Book of Revelation: "I saw a great white throne, and Him who sat on it. . . . And I saw the dead, small and great, standing before God, and books were opened. . . . And the dead were judged according to their works. . . . And Death and Hades were cast into the lake of fire. This is the second death. And anyone not found written in the Book of Life was cast into the lake of fire" (20:11-12, 14-15).

Are you ready for His coming? Do you look and long for the speedy return of your Savior and Lord? If so, then remain faithful; keep witnessing and working; keep looking and hoping. One day you will be home with the Lord. But if you are not ready, then receive Him in repentance and faith. Commit your life into His keeping, and you will find that life now takes on new meaning as you walk each day with Him, and you, too, will inwardly long for His return to take you home with Him forever.

9

WHAT JESUS MEANS TO ME

Key verse: "For to me to live is Christ" (Phil. 1:21, KJV).

After 55 years of speaking and studying about Christ, I'm not bored or tired. It gets more thrilling all the time. I don't lecture on what Socrates or Confucius means to me but what Jesus means to me. He is the most baffling, intriguing, and exciting figure in history. He is the only One I can preach about from Sunday to Sunday, year after year, without getting tired of speaking about Him. Neither do the people get tired of hearing about Him.

What does Jesus mean to me?

In His life, He is my example. Jesus came preaching a new order on earth: God's order, the kingdom of God. He declared that the first commandment is to love God with all the heart, mind, soul, and strength, and that the second is to love our neighbor as ourselves. His teaching is unequaled for the purity of its ethics. He taught that it is not enough to do a good deed, but that it must be done with the right motive and in the right spirit. To pray, fast, or give alms just to be seen by people, He said, is a mockery and a farce. He taught that wrong attitudes and wrong desires are, in God's sight, just as sinful as wrong actions and wrong words. He equated lust with adultery, anger with murder. He emphasized inner purity. He said that we must first *be* good before we can *do* good. He taught us to love our enemies, to pray for those who abuse us, to turn the other cheek if smitten on one side.

Jesus is my example of holiness. Though in a world steeped in sin, sin would not lay its ugly hand upon His spotless robe. Though tempted in all points as we are, He never yielded to a single temptation. He was not made impure by contact with sinful people; on the other hand, they were made pure by His impact. There was no tear of penitence on His cheek, no prayer for forgiveness on His lips. He met all tests and trials victoriously. He challenged all people to convict Him of sin. Friend and foe alike testified to His sinlessness. He said, "He who has seen Me has seen the Father" (John 14:9). On the lips of anyone else this would be terrible blasphemy, but coming from His lips, it is infinite reality. Jesus is the Man who gave God a good reputation.

Jesus is also my example in service. He said, "If anyone desires to be first, he shall be last of all and servant of all" (Mark 9:35). "He who loses his life for My sake will find it" (Matt. 10:39). Though He was the Creator, the Son of God, He said, "The Son of Man did not come to be served, but to serve" (Mark 10:45). He lived for others—for the poor, the sick, the lonely, the discouraged, the sinful. On the night of His arrest, He took a towel and washed the feet of His disciples.

With Jesus as my example, I need never go wrong.

When my brother and I were missionaries in India, one day we dropped into an urban restaurant for midmorning refreshments. When the waiter handed us the menu, we were astonished to see on the top in bold letters, "Give yourself a breakdown—drink our coffee." We asked the waiter about this strange kind of advertisement, and he explained that the original menu read, "Give yourself a break—drink our coffee." But one day a prankster wrote on his menu, after the word "break," the word "down." Later on, the restaurant ran out of menus, so they ordered a reprint. Unfortunately, the copy of the menu they sent to the printers as the model was the one on which the prankster had written the word "down." So all the menus came back from the print shop with "Give yourself a breakdown—drink our coffee." They had the wrong model, it all went wrong.

The only perfect model or example in life is the Lord Jesus Christ. If we follow Him, we will never go wrong. He will never let us down.

In His death, Jesus is my redemption. Christ died one of the most shameful and cruel deaths in all history. He was crucified on a cross between two thieves. His death was the crime of all crimes, the tragedy of all tragedies. And yet today the symbol of shame and suffering—the Cross—has become the supreme symbol of the Christian faith. We build crosses on our churches, place them on our altars, and wear them around our necks. Artists portray the Cross on canvas, poets describe Christ's death on the Cross, hymn writers sing of it, and preachers proclaim it from their pulpits. Jesus took the Cross and turned it into our redemption. He took suffering and turned it into salvation. He took rejection and turned it into reconciliation.

Jesus could do this because He was more than man; He was the God-Man. He was God in human flesh. The Cross was not just martyrdom; it was not simply the end of a man who died for a good cause. It was the sacrifice of God for the sins of humanity. The Cross was not a picture of Christ in trouble, but a picture of God in action.

If Jesus were just a man, then his death was *murder,*
If He were God, then His death was a *sacrifice.*
If he were just a man, then they *took his life* from him;
If He were God, then He *laid down His life* of His own will.
If he were just a man, then I give him my *admiration;*
If He be God, then I give Him my *adoration.*
If he be just a man, then I *take off my hat* to him;
If He be God, then I kneel and *give Him my heart.*
—From *They Met at Calvary*
by W. E. Sangster

When I look at the Cross, I see myself as God sees me. I see that darkness of my heart and the awfulness of my sin. I see my pride, unbelief, disobedience, and folly. I see that it was *my* sins that nailed Him to the Cross. Again, when I look at the Cross, I see God's matchless love for me. I see that He cared enough to come to earth to live and to die for me. Through the wounds of Jesus I look straight into the heart of God, and I cry out, "I didn't know You loved me like that!" And at the foot of the Cross I find forgiveness for all my sins, cleansing from all my impurity, strength for all my weakness.

In His death, Christ is my redemption.

In His resurrection, Christ is my victory. I read the wonderful life of Jesus in the Gospels, a life of purity and service. I listen to His teachings and message, and I say, "Never did anyone speak like this Man." I say with all my heart, "This Man alone is worthy to be my Teacher and my Example. I will follow Him to the death."

Then I stand at the foot of the Cross and see Him dying for my sins. I know He is innocent, sinless, but He is taking my place and suffering by death, and I say, "Does God care for me that much? Does He love me to that extent?" And I am deeply grateful to Him for what He has done for me on the Cross.

But then I see them taking His body down from the Cross and burying Him in a borrowed tomb. Now I am puzzled. Is this the end?

Has Christ gone the way of all flesh—dust to dust, ashes to ashes? Is death the final word? Is the grave conqueror over all? If so, my deepest hopes are shattered. This man, wonderful though He was, is after all just a man—yes, a noble man, the best among men, but only a man. He is just a memory, just a passing figure in history.

But as I am still musing, suddenly I see a great light envelop the tomb. I see the stone moving. The tomb is open. I rush in and look at the place where they laid Him. But the body is gone! Not only did they kill Him, but now they have stolen His body. Now not even His grave can be a hallowed place of memory, for it is a grave without a body.

I walk slowly out of the tomb and down through the garden. This is too much to bear. And suddenly I hear a voice behind me say, "J. T." I turn and look into the face of Jesus. I fall at His feet and cry out, "My Lord and my God!" And now I know that He truly is God. He is not just a fleeting figure in history; He is the Lord of all time. He has conquered our last enemy—even death. So I cry out with Paul, "O death, where is thy sting? O grave, where is thy victory?" (1 Cor. 15:55, KJV).

The resurrection of Christ is the only event that I can know personally, experientially. I was not living when He was upon earth; I did not see Him die. But I have met Him as the living Lord!

So if you were to ask me, "How do you know that Christ is alive?" I could answer with full confidence, "I know He lives because He lives in me. I spoke to Him just this morning."

In His resurrection, Christ is my victory.

In His return, Christ is my hope. I look all around me and see injustice, suffering, pain, and war. I see nations rise and fall, institutions crumble, change on every hand. I wonder if there is anything really dependable, unchangeable, secure. Then I hear the Word say, "Jesus Christ is the same yesterday, today, and forever" (Heb. 13:8). And I realize that I belong to an unchanging Christ and an everlasting Kingdom! I hear Jesus say, "In My Father's house are many mansions. . . . I will come again and receive you to Myself; that where I am, there you may be also" (John 14:2-3). Then I know that He will have the last word in history. I know that His kingdom shall endure forever. And this is my abiding hope.

During World War II when things looked bleak for England and the Allies, in a particular town in England the people were putting on a special program of entertainment, seeking to raise money for the war fund. An attractive little girl with beautiful curly hair was walking around selling a variety of trinkets. One gentleman in the audience was so fascinated with her poise and zeal that, when she came by, he said to her, "Little girl, tell me—what do you think about the future of the war?"

Without a moment's hesitation, she threw back her head, looked the man straight in the eye, and said in a loud, clear voice, "Sir, our king says there is hope!"

With all the turmoil, strife, bloodshed, and suffering going on in the world today, you may ask me, "What do you think about the future?"

I answer with all confidence, "Friend, our King says there is hope!" He is coming again to set up His kingdom.

10

WHAT JESUS DID FOR ME

It is helpful now and then just to stop and think seriously about what the Savior has done for us. No danger was too great, no sacrifice too exacting for Him to undergo for our redemption. He gave His very all; not a mite did He withhold. When we catch a glimpse of His immeasurable love and untold sacrifice, we will learn to love Him more and try to serve Him more faithfully. In return for His big all, we will want to give our little all. "Jesus paid it all; / All to Him I owe" will become the theme song of our lives.

As a basis for our meditation on this subject, I want to use a series of rhyme words that will help to indelibly impress upon our minds what Christ has done for us: Satan *fought* me, but Jesus *sought* me, He *bought* me, He *caught* me, He *brought* me, and He *taught* me.

Satan *fought* me. It was God's will and desire that I be saved and transformed. He did all in His power to redeem and woo me to himself. But Satan attempted to frustrate God's plan for me. He fought against God and against me. He tried to stifle the voice of conscience, to dull my sensibility to sin, to bind me with the chain of evil habits. He endeavored to sow seeds of doubt in my mind and get me to postpone making a decision for Christ. He tried to lure me with the pleasures of this world and made many false promises to me. Sometimes Satan came as a roaring lion to frighten and intimidate; sometimes he came as an angel of light to deceive and lead astray. He made a great effort to mar my life and destroy my soul.

But the Master was on my side. He stood up for me and battled on my behalf. He never gave up on me. Praise His name!

Jesus *sought* me. "The Son of Man has come to seek and to save that which was lost" (Luke 19:10). Whether as the sheep, through carelessness, or as the coin, through the carelessness of someone else, or as the son, through willful disobedience, I was lost—yet Jesus sought me. Like the shepherd, He climbed the steeps and dared the jagged precipice in order to bring me back to the fold. Like the anxious housewife, He cleaned house to find me and restore me to His possession. Like the patient, loving father, He ran out to meet me and take me in His arms as His own son once again.

After a bloody and costly battle one day during the United States Civil War, an aged father received word that his beloved son had fallen wounded on the battlefield. Forgetting his weakness and all danger, the old gentlemen hobbled on his cane toward the field of battle and wandered among the dead and wounded for hours in search of his son. Night came, and still he saw no trace of the wounded lad. The weary father lit a lantern and continued his search, allowing the light of the lantern to fall on the faces of the dead and wounded. At last, at midnight, he came upon his wounded son, lying in a pool of blood. With great difficulty the father hoisted his son onto his back and trudged the way back home, repeating to himself as he went, "My son is found. My son is found." How like the Master, who sought us when we lay wounded and defeated on the battlefield of life and brought us home to safety.

He *bought* me. "You are not your own . . . you were bought at a price" (1 Cor. 6:19-20), writes the apostle Paul. Jesus not only sought me but bought me with His precious blood. He purchased my redemption at tremendous cost. Henceforth, I belong to Him, and if I withhold anything, I'm robbing Him of what rightfully belongs to Him.

Some things we buy to sell, and some things we buy to keep and use. Jesus bought me for keeps, to make me His own and to use me in His service. He didn't buy me to make me His slave and order me about, but He bought me to set me free from the bondage of sin and bestow upon me the honor of being a child of His.

He *caught* me. Not by force or trickery, but He caught me by the sheer power of His love. When I realized His great sacrifice for me and felt His look of compassion upon me, every barrier was broken down. Jesus caught me in His arms of love. As in the words of Major John André,

> *Against the God who built the sky*
> *I fought with hands uplifted high,*
> *Despised the mention of His grace,*
> *Too proud to seek a hiding place.*

> *And thus the eternal counsel ran:*
> *"Almighty love, arrest that man!"*
> *I felt the arrows of disgrace,*
> *And found I had no hiding place.*

He *brought* me. "Christ also suffered once for sins, the just for the unjust, that He might *bring* us to God" (1 Pet. 3:18, emphasis added). . . . "He also *brought* me up out of a horrible pit, out of the miry clay, and set my feet upon a rock, and established my steps" (Ps. 40:2, emphasis added). When I was sinking in the mire of sin, the Savior reached down with His strong arms of love and brought me out. When I was wandering away from the fold, the Good Shepherd sought me and brought me back to His shelter and safety. He brought me from sin to righteousness, from darkness to light, from bondage to freedom, from death to life.

He *taught* me. "Take My yoke upon you and learn from Me" (Matt. 11:29) is the Master's loving invitation. He taught me the destructive power of sin and the constructive power of right. He taught me to live in God and to realize that God is to live in me. "He taught me how to watch and pray, / And live rejoicing every day." Daily I sit at His feet in the quiet hour and learn new and deeper truths of spiritual things. Everything He teaches me is for my good and growth. Truly He is the Master Teacher.

And so this is what Jesus has done for me. He *sought* me when I was straying; He *bought* me with His precious blood; He *caught* me in His arms of love; He *brought* me back to the fold; and He *taught* me to trust and obey. And now He whispers softly to me,

> *I gave, I gave My life for thee.*
> *What hast thou giv'n for Me?*
> —Frances R. Havergal

Rabindranath Tagore, famous poet of India, told the story of a miserable old beggar who daily stood on a roadside to ask money from passersby. His clothes were tattered and torn, his face unshaven. With one hand he leaned upon a staff; in the other he held a brass bowl.

On this particular day he was tired and discouraged. He had been standing by the roadside almost the whole day, but there were only a few copper coins in his bowl and a little bit of rice. His luck had been very poor. Evening was drawing near, and he debated whether he should start for home.

But just then he looked down the road and in the distance saw a cloud of dust. After some time he could see that the rajah (king) of the land was driving in his direction, seated upon his golden chariot and surrounded by a mounted guard. The beggar soon forgot how tired he was, for he realized that this was the chance of a lifetime. He had often heard of the generosity of the rajah, and he said to himself, *As soon as the chariot comes near, I'll step forward and ask alms from the rajah. Maybe he'll have pity upon my awful condition and give me a large amount of money—maybe gold—or perhaps even land. Then I'll never need to beg again; I can live happily the rest of my life.* So very anxiously he watched the chariot as it came closer and closer.

At last the chariot was directly in front of the beggar. He stepped forward and held out his bowl. But before he could say a word, the rajah suddenly stepped down from his chariot and, approaching the beggar, said, "Friend, what do you have to give to me?"

The beggar was taken by complete surprise. He should be asking alms from the rajah, but here was the rajah asking a gift from him. What had he to give? Again the rajah said, "Friend, what do you have to give to me?"

So the poor man reached into his bowl, took out a single grain of rice, and placed it into the hand of the rajah. The rajah then ascended his chariot and in a short while was out-of-sight. The poor beggar hung his head. He was still a beggar, with nothing but his torn clothes and little bowl.

When he reached his hut, the beggar turned over his bowl to gather the grains of rice and count his few coins. To his surprise, there in the midst of the grains of rice was a small shiny object. He picked it up and looked at it. It was a piece of pure gold, exactly the same size and shape as the grain of rice he had given to the rajah. Then he came to his senses. "What a fool I've been!" he cried. "If only I had given everything in my bowl to the rajah, my bowl would have been filled with gold. I've missed the chance of a lifetime!"

Jesus is saying to us today, "What do you have to give to Me?" If we give our little all to Him, He will give us His big all.

11

WHAT JESUS BELIEVED

We want to know what Jesus believed when He walked among us, because that is exactly what *we* should believe. We cannot go astray when we follow Him. He is the perfect example. But more than that, He himself gives the power to believe and do as we should. He is both example and empowerer. He goes *before* us to *lead* the way and lives *within* us to keep us *in* the way.

Just what did Jesus demonstrate that He believed while here on earth? Both by precept and practice He has demonstrated that—

He believed more in *mercy* than in *might;*

He believed that *love* is stronger than *law;*

He believed that *service* is greater than *status;*

He believed that *faith* is greater than *fear.*

He believed more in mercy than in might. Jesus said, "Whoever slaps you on your right cheek, turn the other to him also. . . . Bless those who curse you, do good to those who hate you, and pray for those who spitefully use you and persecute you" (Matt. 5:39, 44). On the night of Christ's arrest He didn't call Judas, "you low-down betrayer," but He called him "friend" and offered him, along with the other disciples, the bread and cup. When Peter tried to defend Him with a sword, Jesus didn't say to Peter, "Good for you, Peter—hit him again!" Instead, He said, "Peter, put up your sword," and then He stooped to heal the wounded ear.

A young Christian soldier knelt by his bedside in prayer one night in the barracks. A half-drunken, cursing colleague mocked at his piety and flung his heavy boots at the kneeling form. The Christian never said a word but finished his prayer and then crawled into bed for the night. In the morning, the soldier who had thrown his dirty, mud-stained boots at the Christian soldier found his boots shined and polished and neatly placed by his bed. When he discovered that it was the Christian who had shined the boots, his hard heart melted in repentance and he came to the young man for forgiveness and spiritual help.

What retaliation and aggression could not have done, mercy accomplished in swift silence.

Look at Saul, blind and broken, as he prayed in a home in Damascus. When Ananias came to call on him, Ananias did not say, "You murderer! You blasphemer!" Instead, he began, "Brother Saul" (Acts 9:17). How these two words must have melted the heart of one who had been responsible for the death of hundreds and even now had been on his way to kill many others!

Jesus said, "Blessed are the merciful, for they shall obtain mercy" (Matt. 5:7).

Jesus believed that love is stronger than law. When the scribes and Pharisees brought a woman taken in adultery and stood her before the Master, saying, "Moses, in the law, commanded us that such should be stoned. But what do You say?" (John 8:5). Our Lord was not interested in fulfilling the letter of the Law. He was not interested in sheer justice. He was interested in redeeming the woman and restoring her to a life of purity and usefulness. So He said to the crowd, "He who is without sin among you, let him throw a stone at her first" (v. 7), and to the woman he said, "Neither do I condemn you; go and sin no more" (v. 11).

Recall Jesus' parable of the Good Samaritan. A Jewish traveler was beaten and robbed. He lay half-dead and forsaken along the roadside. Along came a priest, well versed in the Scriptures, but he passed him by. Then came another priest, thoroughly acquainted with the Temple rituals, but he also passed him by. Finally there came a Samaritan, who belonged to a different ethnic group but was prompted by love to stop and help a man in need. The first two knew the Jewish Law, but the third man knew only love.

It is no wonder, then, that Jesus summed up the entire Law in two greater positive commands: "You shall love the LORD your God with all your heart, with all your soul, and with all your mind" and "You shall love your neighbor as yourself" (Matt. 22:37-39).

Jesus believed that service is greater than status. On one occasion an argument arose among the disciples of Jesus as to who was the greatest among them. When Jesus understood what they were arguing about, He placed a child in front of them and said, "Whoever humbles himself as this little child is the greatest in the kingdom of heaven" (Matt. 18:4).

On another occasion He said to them, "He who is greatest among you shall be your servant" (23:11). He also said, "The Son of Man did not come to be served, but to serve" (Mark 10:45).

On the night of His betrayal, Jesus taught His disciples the greatest lesson in this regard when He arose from the supper table, tied a towel around His waist, and washed His disciples' feet. Here was the Lord of heaven stooping to the most menial task of washing the feet of men. Jesus said, "You call me Teacher and Lord, and you say well, for so I am. If I then, your Lord and Teacher, have washed your feet, you also ought to wash one another's feet. For I have given you an example, that you should do as I have done to you" (John 13:13-15).

Jesus taught all of us that the way to the top is through the towel.

Jesus believed that faith is greater than fear. The only true antidote to fear is faith. That is why, again and again, the Scriptures urge us not to fear, but only believe. Almost every time we are urged not to fear, there follows a promise to strengthen our faith. For example, we read in Isa. 41:10 first the exhortation "Fear not," and then the promise "for I am with you." Again, "Be not dismayed," followed by "for I am your God. I will strengthen you."

Jesus was constantly dispelling fear with faith. When everyone had given up hope for the healing of Jairus's daughter, Jesus said, "Do not be afraid; only believe" (Mark 5:36). And faith brought the girl up from the dead.

When the disciples were fearful of coming persecution and opposition, Jesus said, "Do not fear therefore; you are of more value than many sparrows. Therefore whoever confesses Me before men, him I will also confess before My Father who is in heaven" (Matt. 10:31-32). When they were worried about material needs, about food and clothing, He said to them, "Do not worry about your life, what you will eat; nor about the body, what you will put on. . . . Your Father knows that you need these things. But seek the kingdom of God, and all these things shall be added to you" (Luke 12:22, 30-31). When upset with the cares of the world, they heard the Master say, "Do not fear, little flock, for it is your Father's good pleasure to give you the kingdom" (v. 32).

Jesus has been speaking these words down through the years. He is God's answer to the world's gloom, despondency, and pessimism. Are you afraid of your sins? "Fear not," He says. "I am able to save to the uttermost." Are you afraid of the world, the powers of evil? "Fear not," he says. "I have overcome the world." Are you afraid of your own weakness? "Fear not," He says. "All things are possible to him who believes." Are you afraid of life's changes and uncertainties? "Fear not," He says. "The Father has put all things into My hands." Are you afraid of death? "Fear not," He says. "I am the resurrection and the life."

Yes, Jesus believed that mercy is greater than might, love is stronger than law, service is greater than status, and faith is stronger than fear. He believed it. He demonstrated it. He proved it. Let us also believe and practice the same.

12

THE ſPIRIT OF JEſUſ

Scripture passage: Matt. 9:35-38

> Jesus went about all the cities and villages, teaching in their synagogues, preaching the gospel of the kingdom, and healing every sickness and every disease among the people. But when He saw the multitudes, He was moved with compassion for them, because they were weary and scattered, like sheep having no shepherd. Then He said to His disciples, "The harvest truly is plentiful, but the laborers are few. Therefore pray the Lord of the harvest to send out laborers into His harvest."

Key verse: "But when He saw the multitudes, He was moved with compassion for them" (v. 36).

In the key verse three statements are made about Jesus:

First, He *saw.*

Second, He *felt.*

Third, He *acted.*

The fact that He saw suggests *vision.* That He felt suggests *compassion.* That He acted suggests *consecration.* Three great missionary lessons thus stand out boldly in the Scripture lesson:

The need of vision.

The need of compassion.

The need of consecrated action.

Vision—"He Saw the Multitudes"

Note first the *content* of Christ's vision. It was more than physical sight—it was spiritual understanding. He saw beyond the exterior and the veneer. He saw beyond color and creed. Jesus saw not just a crowd of people but individuals fainting, scattered, without a leader. He saw

71

people as persons—persons worth giving himself for, persons worth redeeming. He saw people not as they were, but as they *could* be by the grace of God.

Recall for a moment the incident at the well of Sychar. The disciples saw only a woman who had come to draw water; Jesus saw a sinful woman in need of the water of life. They saw the well as a place of rest; Jesus saw it as a place of revival. While they were getting lunch, He started the revival.

The Savior saw people in *physical need.* He had a sharp eye for the miserable leper. He had an alert ear for the cry of the blind. He had a ready hand for the sick and the hungry. But Jesus saw beyond the outer physical to the inner *spiritual needs.* He saw the sinful, the lonely, the tempted, the discouraged.

What we see will, of course, determine what we do. Years ago, the Singer Company saw many villages in third world countries without any means of sewing cloth and set about to put a sewing machine in every village. The Church sees cities and villages without Christ and has set out to get the gospel to every area of the world.

Note the *extent* of Christ's vision. He saw intensely. He saw the lost, the last, and the least. But He also saw extensively—He saw the multitudes, the plentiful harvest. He saw the whole world. Though He never set foot out of the tiny land of Palestine, He saw the vast continents, the countless islands, the teeming cities, the isolated villages. He commanded, "Go into all the world and preach the gospel" (Mark 16:15). "Go therefore and make disciples of all the nations" (Matt. 28:19). He declared, "I, if I be lifted up from the earth, will draw all men unto me" (John 12:32, KJV).

Our vision is so limited, so selfish, so prejudiced, so distorted. We think only of ourselves, our group, or our own nation. We need a worldwide vision that will go beyond all these boundaries and will take in the whole world. We need the spirit of John Wesley that prompted him to say, "The world is my parish."

A young lad of 12 was called upon to pray at the vespers service in a mission boarding school in India. In the middle of his prayer he suddenly remembered that next week was exam week, so he prayed, "Lord, help me to pass the exam next week." But realizing he should pray not only for himself, he prayed, "Lord, help everyone in my class to pass the exam." But still he felt he had not gone far enough, so he prayed, "Lord, help everyone in the whole school to pass." But he was still not satisfied, so he continued, "Lord, help everyone in all the schools to pass." After a brief pause, his vision seemed to mount still higher, so he cried out, "Lord, let the whole world pass!" In the same way our spiritual vision should be enlarged so as to prompt us to pray, "Lord, let the whole world hear of Christ and come to know Him."

Compassion—"He Was Moved with Compassion"

Christ was not simply touched for a moment with mild pity. His heart was moved to its very depths. He actually suffered in His compassion for people. His heart broke and bled for sorrowing and sinning humanity. He was called "a Man of sorrows and acquainted with grief," because He bore the grief and carried the sorrows of others. His compassion led to an all-consuming passion, a lifelong concern. Jesus had one desire, one task, one goal: to seek and to save the lost.

Today we seem to have lost our concern, our passion for souls. We seem to be more interested in raising the budget, paying the apportionments, and running the machinery of the church than we are in seeking lost men and women, boys and girls. To a great extent, we have lost the love of preaching and the art of bringing a person to Christ. We need to recapture the passion of the great pioneers.

Moses prayed forgiveness for his people, "but if not, I pray, blot me out of Your book" (Exod. 32:32). Henry Martin, as he stepped ashore in India, said, "Now let me burn out for God." David Livingstone of Africa cried, "I will open a way to the interior or perish." Hudson Taylor, speaking with great emotion, said, "I feel as if I could not live if something is not done for China." John Knox cried out from the depths of his soul, "Give me Scotland or I die." David Brainerd declared, "I care not where I go or what hardships I endure, so long as I can see souls won to Christ. When I sleep I dream of these, and when I awake, it is my first thought. All my desire is the conversion of souls, and all my hope is in God."

How deeply do you and I feel about the needy and the lost?

Action—"He Was Moved"

"He went about . . . teaching . . . preaching . . . healing."

Jesus not only saw and felt but also acted. Emotion is never a satisfactory substitute for action. True compassion pours itself out in service. The only compassion that is real and that counts is the compassion that gives itself in some tangible way, in some practical effort, for the good and for the redemption of others. It is said of Jesus that He "went about doing good" (Acts 10:38). Concerning many of us, it may truthfully be said that we "simply went about."

Christ is calling us to action today. He calls us to *pray,* to remember the lost before the throne of grace, to intercede for them at the mercy seat. He calls us to *give,* for every one of us can give something, even though not all in the same measure. We ought to realize that money should not be merely something with which to cater to selfish pleasure and adornment, but something to invest in winning souls to Christ. He calls upon us to *witness,* for though not all are pastors or trained evangelists, each one of us can testify to the saving power of God in his or her own life and recommend the Savior to those who don't know Him. He calls us to *go* as His ambassadors into homes, workplaces, schools, offices, and churches, demonstrating the goodness and holiness of God, reconciling the world to the Father.

Lord, give us the ability to see with the eyes of Jesus, to feel with the heart of Jesus, and to serve with the power of Jesus.

13

THE HANDS OF JESUS

Scripture passage: John 20:19-29

The same day at evening, being the first day of the week, when the doors were shut where the disciples were assembled, for fear of the Jews, Jesus came and stood in the midst, and said to them, "Peace be with you." Now when He had said this, He showed them His hands and His side. Then the disciples were glad when they saw the Lord.

Then Jesus said to them again, "Peace to you! As the Father has sent Me, I also send you." And when He had said this, He breathed on them, and said to them, "Receive the Holy Spirit. If you forgive the sins of any, they are forgiven them; if you retain the sins of any, they are retained."

But Thomas, called Didymus, one of the twelve, was not with them when Jesus came. The other disciples therefore said to him, "We have seen the Lord."

But he said to them, "Unless I see in His hands the print of the nails, and put my finger into the print of the nails, and put my hand into His side, I will not believe."

And after eight days His disciples were again inside, and Thomas with them. Jesus came, the doors being shut, and stood in the midst, and said, "Peace to you!" Then He said to Thomas, "Reach your finger here, and look at My hands; and reach your hand here, and put it into My side. Do not be unbelieving, but believing."

And Thomas answered and said to Him, "My Lord and my God!"

Jesus said to him, "Thomas, because you have seen Me, you have believed. Blessed are those who have not seen and yet have believed."

Key verse: "Look at My hands" (v. 27).

Jesus stands among us today and invites us to look at His hands. By doing so we shall discover something of the character and nature of our Savior. They are wonderful, matchless hands. When we have looked upon them, we will never be the same.

A cowboy listened in rapt attention to the description of Jesus entering into Jerusalem, riding on a colt, and when it was finished, he exclaimed, "What wonderful hands Jesus must have had!"

Someone overheard and asked, "Why do you say that?"

The cowboy answered, "Anyone who can ride a young colt that had never been ridden before—in the middle of a big crowd with all that noise—must have wonderful hands!"

Let us look carefully at these wonderful hands of Jesus and catch a glimpse of His unique character and work. What kind of hands does Jesus have?

Jesus Has Saving Hands—Matt. 14:25-33

The disciples were in a boat one night on the Sea of Galilee when Jesus started walking across the water toward them. Peter decided he would walk on the water and meet Jesus, so he stepped out of the boat and began to walk. But after a few steps, he looked around, saw the wind and waves, became afraid, and began to sink. Then he cried out, "Lord, save me!" Now notice verse 31—"Immediately Jesus *stretched out His hand* and caught him" (emphasis added). If Jesus had not reached out and caught Peter at that moment, Peter would have drowned in the Sea of Galilee. But Jesus rescued him.

Jesus has saving hands. Down through the centuries countless people have been drowning in the sea of sin and guilt, but they have cried out, "Lord, save me!" and Jesus has stretched forth His hand of love and power and delivered them out of a life of sin. Many others have been drowning in the sea of sorrow and despair, but they have called out for help, and Jesus has given them peace and hope.

I will never forget the testimony of a new convert from Hinduism, given just prior to his receiving baptism. He gave his witness in the form of a parable.

"Dear friends," he said, "I had fallen into a very deep pit, and there was no way of escape. The harder I tried to get out, the deeper I went into the pit. Then one day I looked up and saw a man pass by. I cried out, 'Friend, help me! Pull me out of this pit!' He looked down at me and said, 'My friend, this is the result of your *karma*, the evil deeds of your previous existence. Just do the best you can now, do good deeds, and in some future existence you will get out of this pit.' And so saying he went on his way. That was the voice of *Hinduism*.

"Then I looked up and saw another man passing by. I cried, 'Friend, help me! Pull me out of this pit!' He came and looked down at me and said, 'This is the result of desire. You must get rid of all desires, and then you will escape from the pit.' I said, 'Friend, I have only one desire, and that is to get out of this predicament.' But the man went on his way. That was the voice of *Buddhism*.

"I saw a third man passing by, and once again I cried out for help. He looked down at me and said, 'You must do good works. Pray five times a day, give alms to the poor, recite the creed every day, fast one month in the year, and make a pilgrimage to Mecca.' And so saying, he went on his way. That was the voice of *Islam*.

"Finally, one day I looked up and saw another man passing by. I cried out for help, 'Friend, save me from this pit!' He never said a word to me, but with a strong and loving hand He reached down and caught me and lifted me out of the pit. He put my feet on solid rock and put a song of praise in my mouth. That person was my Savior, Jesus Christ!"

Jesus has saving hands. Today if you will realize your condition, repent of your sins, and call out for help, Jesus will lift you out of sin and change your life completely.

Jesus Has Cleansing Hands—Matt. 3:11-12

John the Baptist said to the people one day, "I indeed baptize you with water unto repentance, but He who is coming after me . . . will baptize you with the Holy Spirit and fire." Now notice this: *"His winnowing fan is in His hand,* and He will thoroughly purge His threshing floor, and gather His wheat into the barn; but He will burn up the chaff with unquenchable fire" (emphasis added).

This is an Eastern picture of a farmer sifting the grain at harvesttime. He puts the grain into his winnowing fan, then holds it up and lets the grain fall to the ground. The chaff, because it is lighter, is blown to one side by the wind; then it is burned in the fire.

Jesus not only delivers us from sinful acts but also can cleanse us from our sinful disposition. He puts us in the winnowing fan and sifts us, removing all the chaff and leaving only the pure wheat. He does this through the purifying fire of the Holy Spirit.

Look for a moment at the lives of the disciples before and after

Pentecost. Before Pentecost they were true disciples. They had forsaken all to follow Jesus. Their names were written in the Lamb's Book of Life. They were "not of the world." But still they were suffering from the sins of the disposition. There was the chaff of *pride*. They argued about who was the greatest among them. There was the chaff of *self-seeking*. They sought for thrones and scepters and wanted to sit on the right and left of Jesus and rule in His kingdom. There was the chaff of *jealousy*. They saw some men casting out demons in the name of Jesus, but they didn't belong to the inner circle. So they asked Jesus to restrain them. There was also the chaff of *anger* in their lives. They wanted to call down fire from heaven and burn up the Samaritans, because they would not grant them hospitality for the night.

But one memorable day something happened in the hearts of the disciples. The Holy Spirit came in His fullness and like fire burned up all the chaff in their lives, leaving only the pure wheat. Instead of pride, there was now humility. Instead of selfishness, there was now self-giving. In place of jealousy, there was kindness and consideration. Hatred gave way to love.

Jesus has cleansing hands. He is able to lift us out of sin and also to take sin out of us.

Jesus Has Protecting Hands—John 10:11, 27-28

Jesus said, "I am the good shepherd. . . . My sheep hear My voice, and I know them, and they follow Me. And I give them eternal life, and they shall never perish." Then note carefully: "neither shall anyone snatch them *out of My hand*" (emphasis added).

By His strong hand Jesus is able not only to *save* us but also to *keep* us from day to day. We are safe as long as we abide in Him, as long as we stay in His hands. We need not fear the trials and temptations of life; we need not be overcome by the stress and strain of the world. *Nothing* can separate us from the love of Christ.

A young lad used to walk to school every day in India. But on the way he was often accosted by a bigger boy who was a bully and played all sorts of pranks on him. So in desperation, the young lad started going a roundabout way to school in order to avoid the bullying. One day his older brother came home from college on vacation. The next morning the young boy said to his brother, "Please walk with me to school today. I would appreciate it." So the two started off together, but this day the young boy did not take the roundabout way. He went straight down the road, past the house of the bully. He was not afraid. When the bully saw him, he wanted to play tricks on him as usual; but when he saw the strong, athletic older brother, the bully was afraid to touch the young lad.

Before Christ saves us, the devil acts like a big bully, making life miserable for us. He orders us around and makes slaves out of us. But when we accept Christ as our Savior, Christ becomes our elder Brother. He now takes us by the hand and leads us safely through life. No one is able to snatch us out of His hand.

Jesus Has Wounded Hands—John 20:20, 27

"He showed them His hands and His side. . . . He said to Thomas, 'Reach your finger here, and *look at My hands;* and reach your hand here, and put it into My side. Do not be unbelieving, but believing.'"

And now we see Jesus on the Cross with His arms stretched out. Hands that once rescued and set people free are now bound tightly. Hands that once brought comfort and health are now full of pain and suffering. Hands that once hammered nails into wood in the carpenter's shop are now fastened by nails into the wood of the Cross. Hands that once healed a woman from an issue of blood are now dripping with their own blood.

Why all this agony and shame? The prophet Isaiah gives us the answer: "He was wounded for our transgressions, He was bruised for our iniquities; the chastisement for our peace was upon Him, and by His stripes we are healed. . . . The LORD has laid on Him the iniquity of us all" (Isa. 53:5-6). When we look at the hands of Jesus, we know that He suffered for our sins.

In India lived a mother who had very ugly hands. They were so scarred and repulsive that her young daughter was often embarrassed in public when people saw them. She often said, "Mama, you have such ugly hands. Please put them behind your back. I don't like to look at them."

One day when the daughter spoke in this fashion, her mother set her down on a chair and said to her, "I want to tell you about my hands. I used to have nice hands at one time, but one day when I was cooking in the kitchen and you were crawling around on the floor, there was a knock at the door. I went to see who it was. While I was talking with the person, I heard a sudden scream from the kitchen, and I came running. I saw that you had crawled too close to the open fireplace, and your clothes were on fire. Immediately with my hands I tore the clothes from your body and beat out the flames. But in doing so, my hands were terribly burned. It took a long time for them to heal, and to this day they are scarred and ugly."

When the daughter heard this, she began to weep. Then she reached out and took hold of her mother's hands, kissed them tenderly, and said "Mother, what beautiful hands you have!"

When we look at the hands of Jesus on the Cross, there is no outward beauty in them. They are bleeding and lifeless. They are scarred and ugly. But when we realize that Jesus was suffering for our sins, then we cry out in gratitude, "Jesus, what beautiful hands You have!" For in those hands there is forgiveness, cleansing, healing, and comfort.

We have looked at the hands of Jesus and found that He has wonderful hands—saving hands, cleansing hands, protecting hands, wounded hands. Now what should we do? We must do exactly what Thomas did when Jesus stood before him in His resurrection power and said to him, "Thomas, look at My hands." When Thomas looked, he fell on his knees and cried out, "My Lord and my God!" And that confession and commitment changed the life of Thomas. He was no longer the doubting, but the daring, disciple. Tradition tells us that Thomas went to India, preached, made disciples, and laid the foundation of a great church that still exists after 1,900 years. Today there are several million Christians in the state of Kerala, in south India, because of the ministry of missionary Thomas. After a few years of service, it is said that Thomas was pierced to death by a Brahman priest with a spear, and his body is said to lie buried in a church in Madras.

We must do the same as Thomas today. Having seen the wonderful hands of Jesus and realizing all they stand for, we must kneel in His presence and exclaim, "My Lord and my God!" That confession will change our lives and send us forth to be witnesses for Christ wherever He sends us.

14

JESUS AT THE DOOR

Scripture passage: Rev. 3:20-21

> Behold, I stand at the door and knock. If anyone hears My voice and opens the door, I will come in to him and dine with him, and he with Me.
>
> To him who overcomes I will grant to sit with Me on My throne, as I also overcame and sat down with My Father on His throne.

Key verse: "Behold, I stand at the door and knock" (v. 20).

Doors play a very important part in our everyday life. One of the first things we do when we get up in the morning is to open the door. One of the last things we do at night before we go to sleep is to close the door. All during the day we are going in and out of doors—house doors, office doors, classroom doors, store doors.

There are a great variety of doors—ordinary house doors, elaborate cathedral doors, revolving doors, automatic electric doors, and so on. But in the passage above we have perhaps the most important of all doors—the door to the human heart. Jesus declares that He is standing at the door of the human heart and is seeking entrance. Everything depends upon whether we open the door and invite Him in or keep the door fast closed and shut Him out of our lives.

Think prayerfully on this dramatic scene of Christ standing at the door.

The Person

Who stands knocking on the door of the human heart? Jesus says, "Behold, *I* stand at the door" (emphasis added). It is not a pastor, a bishop, the pope, or any other human person, but the Lord Jesus himself. The divine striving with the human; the sinless dealing with the sinful; the innocent pleading with the guilty. It is the Christ who went to the Cross, the One who trod the rugged road to Calvary and offered himself as a sacrifice for our sins. He now returns with a cure for sin, a cure purchased by His precious blood. It is this same Christ who keeps vigil at the heart's door.

A certain pastor heard about the financial problems of one of his church members. She was a widow who was unable to pay the house rent and was facing eviction by the landlord. So in compassion the pastor received a generous offering and then went to the lady's house to deliver the gift. He knocked on the front door several times and even called out the lady's name, but there was no response. Disappointed, he left and went home.

The following Sunday the pastor saw the lady in church and told her that he had called on her in order to deliver a gift he had for her. "Oh, was that you knocking on my door?" asked the lady. "I was at home and heard you knock and call my name, but I thought you were the landlord trying to collect the rent. So I pretended I was not at home."

If we realize how important the person is who is knocking at our heart's door, and what it is that He wants to do for us, we will not keep Him standing outside but will gladly let Him in.

His Position

Where is Christ standing? Jesus says, "Behold, I stand *at the door*" (emphasis added). He stands *outside,* when His rightful place is *inside.* What persistency! He stands continually; He knocks unceasingly. He's deeply interested in the person on the inside.

Perhaps you have seen the picture by Holman Hunt titled *The Light of the World.* There is a crown of thorns upon the Savior's head, above it a halo. In one hand he holds a beautiful lantern; with the other He is knocking upon the closed door of a weather-beaten little house, around which weeds and briars have sprung up. If you look carefully at the picture, you will find a star shining brilliantly between the leaves of the tree under which Christ is standing. It is said to be the Morning Star, the artist's way of suggesting something that is not at all overdrawn. It is that Christ has been standing there the whole day and night through, and still there is no response.

That is not an exaggeration. People live all around us at whose door Christ has been standing—not for a day, not for a night, but for weeks, months, and even years. And still He is denied the place in their lives to which He is entitled. Oh, what marvelous patience!

His Petition

What is Christ pleading for?

He pleads first for *attention*—"Hear My voice." An interesting story is told concerning the painting by Holman Hunt. A little Sunday School lad was looking at a print of it. The idea that Jesus was being denied entrance into that heart bothered him. He came to his father with the picture and said, "Daddy, look at this. Why don't they let Him in?"

His father answered, "Son, I don't know, but why are you so uneasy?"

The little fellow thought a moment and then said, "Daddy, I guess they are just so busy in the back part of the house that they don't hear Him."

Preoccupied—that's it. Carried away with other things, listening to other voices. "Will you not listen to My voice?" Christ asks.

He pleads for *attention;* He also pleads for *action:* "Open the door." Hearing is not enough—there must be action. Christ will never force His way in. He is the perfect gentleman. If we ever expect Him to walk across the threshold of our heart's door, we alone must open the door.

It is said that when Holman Hunt finished his great picture, he called in a friend to critique it. The friend was very complimentary but suddenly remarked, "I see one little mistake. You forgot to paint the latch on the door."

"Oh," said Hunt, "I did that on purpose, for the latch is on the *inside.*"

The latch to our heart's door is on the inside. You and I alone must turn the latch and open the door.

His Promise

Jesus' promise is "I will come in to him and dine with him, and he with Me."

First of all, Christ promises His *presence:* "I will come in." What is more precious in life than to have the presence of Christ at all times—guiding, encouraging, strengthening, purifying? He *will* come in. We don't have to beg or entreat Him—just open the door, and He will enter with His matchless personality.

Again, He promises His *joy:* "I will . . . dine with him." This is a picture of fellowship and feasting. He will bring complete satisfaction, lasting joy, and peace. Christ does not come into our lives to rob or impoverish us, but to bless and enrich us. Anything we have to lay aside for Christ's sake will be more than compensated for in the higher satisfaction that Christ will bring to us. He doesn't ask us to give up anything that we wouldn't be better off without, even if we were not His disciples.

Finally, Christ promises His *victory:* "To him who overcomes I will grant to sit with Me on My throne." He has already conquered temptation, sin, and death, so now through Him we can be more than conquerors in every area of life. We don't have to strive *for* the victory; we work *from* the victory that He has already gained.

A young lad was strolling through St. Paul's Cathedral in London with his father when they suddenly came across a life-size painting of *The Light of the World.* The boy looked at it for a while, then asked his father, "Dad, who's that knocking on the door?"

"Son, that's Jesus," replied the father.

"And who's inside?" asked the boy.

"Son, that's anyone. It may be you; it may be me."

The lad was silent for a moment and then said softly to his father, "Dad, if I were inside, I believe I'd let Him in."

Will you fling wide the door today and let Him in? The longer the door stays shut, the harder it will be to open. Let Him come in—you will find His presence and joy and victory more precious than anything the world can offer.

PART 2

The Parables of Jesus

Matthew tells us in his Gospel that Jesus "spoke many things to them in parables" (13:3). The use of the parable was one of His most frequent and effective methods of instructing the people concerning the kingdom of God.

Someone has defined the parable as "an earthly story with a heavenly meaning," and Jesus was certainly the world's supreme Master of the short story. The great teaching value of the parable is that it makes truth concrete; it takes abstract ideas and makes them into beautiful pictures we can see and understand. Love is merely an abstract word until we see a loving person or a loving deed. Beauty is nebulous until we see a beautiful face or a magnificent sunset. The parable puts flesh and shape onto obscure ideas. It also arouses interest and holds the attention of the listener, for people naturally love to hear a good story.

Another virtue of the parable is that it compels the hearers to think and discover truth for themselves. Unless we discover truth for ourselves, it remains secondhand and external and is quickly forgotten. By compelling people to draw their own conclusions, the parable makes truth real to them and fixes it in their memories. At the same time, it conceals truth from those who are either too lazy to think or too blind through prejudice to see. It reveals truth to those who desire to know the truth; it conceals the truth from those who do not wish to see the truth. The responsibility is placed squarely upon the individual.

Having focused in detail thus far on the Person of Jesus, let us now meditate on some of the most well-known and meaningful parables He told. These not only will teach us many spiritual lessons but also will help us know better the One who narrated them.

15

THE GOOD SAMARITAN

Scripture passage: Luke 10:25-37

A certain lawyer stood up and tested Him, saying, "Teacher, what shall I do to inherit eternal life?"

He said to him, "What is written in the law? What is your reading of it?"

So he answered and said, "'You shall love the LORD your God with all your heart, with all your soul, with all your strength, and with all your mind,' and 'your neighbor as yourself.'"

And He said to him, "You have answered rightly; do this and you will live."

But he, wanting to justify himself, said to Jesus, "And who is my neighbor?"

Then Jesus answered and said: "A certain man went down from Jerusalem to Jericho, and fell among thieves, who stripped him of his clothing, wounded him, and departed, leaving him half dead. Now by chance a certain priest came down that road. And when he saw him, he passed by on the other side. Likewise a Levite, when he arrived at the place, came and looked, and passed by on the other side. But a certain Samaritan, as he journeyed, came where he was. And when he saw him, he had compassion on him, and went to him and bandaged his wounds, pouring on oil and wine; and he set him on his own animal, brought him to an inn, and took care of him. On the next day, when he departed, he took out two denarii, gave them to the innkeeper, and said to him, 'Take care of him; and whatever more you spend, when I come again, I will repay you.'

"So which of these three do you think was neighbor to him who fell among the thieves?"

And he said, "He who showed mercy on him."

Then Jesus said to him, "Go and do likewise."

Key verse: "Go and do likewise" (v. 37).

This parable provides a wonderful lesson in contrasts. First of all, there is the contrast in *attitudes*. The attitude of the robbers was "What's yours is mine; I'll take it." The attitude of the priests was "What's mine is mine; I'll keep it." The attitude of the Samaritan was "What's mine is yours; I'll share it." And that is the attitude of the true Christian.

Then there is the contrast in *action*. The robbers said, "We'll *beat* him up." The priests said, "We'll *pass* him up." But the Samaritan said, "I'll *pick* him up."

In this parable Jesus is trying to teach us the Christian attitude toward a world in need. He tells us three things about the attitude of the Christian.

The Christian is one who cares. "When he saw him, he had compassion." Life has been defined as sensitivity. The lowest form of life is sensitive only to itself. The higher you go up the ladder of life, the higher the degree of sensitivity. For instance, the oyster's skeleton is on the outside and its nervous system on the inside. Its shell is its skeleton; it completely encases its nervous system. It opens up only to take in from the outside and then immediately closes up. The human being's skeleton is on the inside, the nervous system on the outside. This is dangerous, because it makes the human person capable of pain and suffering. But it is also his or her glory, because it makes the person sensitive to the environment.

The highest level of sensitivity is found in Jesus Christ. He said to His disciples, "I was hungry and you gave Me food; I was thirsty and you gave Me drink; I was a stranger and you took Me in; I was naked and you clothed Me; I was sick and you visited Me; I was in prison and you came to Me" (Matt. 25:35-36). If we ask, "Lord, when did we do all this?" He answers, "When you did it to others, you did it to Me." Jesus was saying, "I am hungry in everyone's hunger, thirsty in everyone's thirst, bound in everyone's imprisonment." Here is perfect sensitivity and therefore perfect life.

The supreme demonstration of this perfect sensitivity is found in the Cross. Jesus could not say, "I am sinful in your sin," because He was absolutely sinless, but He was sensitive to our sin and did something about it. He went to the Cross and died between two thieves as one of them. He took our place as a sinner and cried the cry of destitution—"My God, My God, why have You forsaken Me?" (27:46). He became sin for us. Here is complete sensitivity.

You can tell how high you have risen on the ladder of life by asking the questions "How highly sensitive am I? How deeply do I care?"

Some people are sensitive only to *themselves*. They ask, "How will this affect me? What do I get out of this?" They are bounded by themselves and are on the lowest rung of life.

Some people are sensitive to their *families*. Anything that strikes a member of the family strikes them. They are a little higher on the ladder, but not much.

Others are sensitive to their own *group*. The laborer is sensitive to what affects the labor world, the manager to what affects the business world, the student to what affects the student body.

Some are sensitive to their own *race,* the Black person to what affects Blacks, the white person to what affects his or her race.

Then some are sensitive to *humanity* as a whole. They feel what strikes anybody, anywhere. They are highest on the ladder.

To be Christianized is to become sensitized. The moment you come into contact with Christ, you begin to care. You come burdened with a sense of your sin and rise a new person. Then you become burdened for the sin and suffering of others.

When Christ transformed me, I wanted to share this new life with everyone. Five minutes before, I had no such impulse. Several years have come and gone since then, but the impulse remains.

Christians become sensitive to the needs of everyone, even those whom they have never met, even their enemies. The people of the Fiji Islands were once cannibals. They killed and ate the first missionaries who entered their land. One of the early missionaries tried to change their attitude. He held up the skull of a man whom they had killed, from which they had drunk his blood, and said to them, "This man was your *brother!*"

The Fijians shook their heads and said, "No, that's a *pig!*" But when Jesus came into their midst, those same people began to care. They stopped the practice of killing and eating one another. When they heard of a famine in far-off India, they sent money to starving people across the seas whom they had never met. They had been sensitized and began to care. No wonder Baron von Hugel defined a Christian as "One who cares."

The Christian is one who shares. When the Samaritan saw the man lying in the ditch, bruised and bleeding, he "went to him and bandaged his wounds, pouring on oil and wine; and he set him on his own animal, brought him to an inn, and took care of him. On the next day, when he departed, he took out two denarii, gave them to the innkeeper, and said to him, 'Take care of him; and whatever more you spend, when I come again, I will repay you'" (Luke 10:34-35).

The Samaritan shared what he had with the man in the ditch—his oil and wine, his donkey, and his money. He gave of his time and energy; he shared himself. Likewise, the Christian is one who cares and shares. Compassion always leads to action. It is not merely standing by the side of the road, looking down at the victim, and saying sadly, "Poor fellow—I feel sorry for him. I wonder what will become of him." Compassion means getting down in the ditch with the victim and helping in every way possible.

When I was a missionary in India, I remember how our South India Annual Conference elected Rev. Y. Samuel as our delegate to the Methodist General Conference in the United States. He landed in New York City in March, and the weather was quite cold. At least it was cold for him, wearing a light cotton suit and no topcoat. He was walking down Fifth Avenue, with his coat collar turned up and his coat pulled tightly around him, when an American businessman, coming from the opposite direction, noticed him. Suddenly the businessman stopped in front of Rev. Samuel and said to him, "Friend, I believe you are from India, are you not? You seem to be cold."

Rev. Samuel replied, "Yes, I am a bit cold. I'm not used to this cold weather."

Right then and there the stranger took off his topcoat, handed it over to Rev. Samuel, and said, "Here—take my coat. I have another one at home."

Rev. Samuel protested, but the American insisted that he keep the coat and then went on his way before Rev. Samuel could even ask his name or address.

When Rev. Samuel returned to India from the General Conference, the thing he talked about the most, wherever he went, was not the majestic skyline of New York City, the supermarkets, or the heavy traffic. The first thing he talked about was the stranger on Fifth Avenue, the man who took off his topcoat and handed it over to him, the man who had compassion on him and shared with him what he had.

The Christian not only shares his worldly possessions with those in need but also shares the good news of Jesus with those who are spiritually in need. For people are not only hungry and need to be fed, not only homeless and need shelter, but spiritually lost and need a Redeemer. They need comfort, purpose, and meaning in life; power to overcome; and hope for the future.

Several years ago an Indian evangelist and I went to a certain village in South India and for several days preached Christ to the outcast section of town. A great revival broke out in the community as the people responded eagerly to the gospel message. They repented of their sins, burned their idols, and dedicated themselves and their homes to the Lord. On the day of our departure, the people escorted us to the edge of the village, and after we had proceeded a short distance, they all raised their hands into the air and kept shouting, "Thank you for bringing Christ to us. Thank you for bringing Christ to us."

The Christian is one who shares his or her goods as well as the Good News with others.

The Christian is one who dares. The Samaritan in the parable dared to break through racial prejudice and custom. He dared to put the beaten man on his donkey, walk alongside, and expose himself to possibly more robbers. He dared to upset his travel schedule and put himself to inconvenience.

The Christian today must dare to leave his or her homeland with its comfort and security, enter a new culture, and expose himself or herself to insecurity, loneliness, danger, nationalism, the threat of persecution, and the criticism of non-Christians. The Christian must dare to proclaim the uniqueness of Christ and the biblical revelation, and call men and women, boys and girls, out of their ancient religions into the gospel of Jesus Christ, out of their sin and into Christ.

Bruce Olson came from a nominal Christian home in Minnesota but in his late teens experienced a radical transformation in his life. At the age of 19 he left home and headed for the South American country of Colombia as a missionary without the support of any organization. Hearing of the fierce Motilone tribe, isolated and without any Christian witness, he decided to make contact with them. He was shot with an arrow by one of the Motilone warriors and was left to die in an open clearing. A helicopter pilot from a nearby oil refinery flew over and, noticing his condition, landed in the clearing, rescued him, and took him to a hospital.

Upon his recovery six weeks later, Olson ventured back into Motilone territory, and this time was received by the tribe. For the past 30 years or so, Bruce Olson has faithfully served these people and preached the gospel to them. Most of them are Christians today, and their whole life has been changed. Bruce introduced agriculture, cattle-raising, medicine, and education to the Motilones, and now they are carrying the gospel to neighboring tribes. Here is the story of a young man who dared to risk his life for the spiritual and social transformation of a whole people because he sincerely cared for them and was willing to share himself with them.

A Christian is one who cares, shares, and dares.

16

LOST BUT FOUND!

Scripture passage: Luke 15:1-24

Then all the tax collectors and the sinners drew near to Him to hear Him. And the Pharisees and scribes murmured, saying, "This man receives sinners and eats with them."

So He spoke this parable to them, saying: "What man of you, having a hundred sheep, if he loses one of them, does not leave the ninety-nine in the wilderness, and go after the one which is lost until he finds it? And when he has found it, he lays it on his shoulders, rejoicing. And when he comes home, he calls together his friends and neighbors, saying to them, 'Rejoice with me, for I have found my sheep which was lost!' I say to you that likewise there will be more joy in heaven over one sinner who repents than over ninety-nine just persons who need no repentance.

"Or what woman, having ten silver coins, if she loses one coin, does not light a lamp, sweep the house, and seek diligently until she finds it? And when she has found it, she calls her friends and neighbors together, saying, 'Rejoice with me, for I have found the piece which I lost!' Likewise, I say to you, there is joy in the presence of the angels of God over one sinner who repents."

Then He said: "A certain man had two sons. And the younger of them said to his father, 'Father, give me the portion of goods that falls to me.' So he divided to them his livelihood.

"And not many days after, the younger son gathered all together, journeyed to a far country, and there wasted his possessions with prodigal living.

"But when he had spent all, there arose a severe famine in that land, and he began to be in want. Then he went and joined himself to a citizen of that country, and he sent him into his fields to feed swine. And he would gladly have filled his stomach with the pods that the swine ate, and no one gave him anything.

"But when he came to himself, he said, 'How many of my father's hired servants have bread enough and to spare, and I perish with hunger! I will arise and go to my father, and will say to him, "Father, I have sinned against heaven and before

you, and I am no longer worthy to be called your son. Make
me like one of your hired servants.'" And he arose and came
to his father.

But when he was still a great way off, his father saw him
and had compassion, and ran and fell on his neck and kissed
him.

"And the son said to him, 'Father, I have sinned against
heaven and in your sight, and am no longer worthy to be
called your son.'

"But the father said to his servants, 'Bring out the best
robe and put it on him, and put a ring on his hand and san-
dals on his feet. And bring the fatted calf here and kill it, and
let us eat and be merry; for this my son was dead and is alive
again; he was lost and is found.' And they began to be merry."

Key verses: "Let us eat and be merry; for this my son was
dead and is alive again; he was lost and is found" (vv.
23-24).

━━━━━━━━━━━━━━━━━━━━━━━━━━━━━━━

The 15th chapter of Luke's Gospel has been called "the lost and
found department of the New Testament." A sheep was lost but was
found; a silver coin was lost but was found; a son was lost but he was
also found. Lost—how tragic! But found—how triumphant!

This chapter has also been called "the gospel in a nutshell." For it
contains enough spiritual truth to convict people of their sins and con-
duct them to the feet of the Savior. Let us now turn our attention to
the three great truths revealed in this parable.

The Twofold Path to Sin

Carelessness

How did the sheep get lost? Through sheer carelessness. It didn't
intend to get lost, but simply drifted away heedlessly. With head toward the ground, it went from green patch to green patch, paying no
attention to the voice of the shepherd and the whereabouts of the other sheep. Little by little it wandered away, until when evening came
and it lifted up its head, the shepherd and remaining sheep were
nowhere to be seen. It was lost.

The silver coin was also lost through carelessness, but not of its
own. It was lost through the carelessness of its owner. The woman of

the house unknowingly dropped it or placed it somewhere and forgot. Then when she wanted a coin, it was nowhere to be seen. It was lost.

Many people are spiritually lost today just from sheer carelessness and neglect. Sometimes it is their own carelessness. They get so busy and preoccupied that they have no time for spiritual things. They say, "I know I should have my quiet time, but this other matter is urgent, so I'll wait until tomorrow" or "I know I should attend church today, but I'm too tired this time—I'll go next Sunday" or "I know this duty is important, but I have no time now—I'll do it later." The tragedy of such thinking is that it tends to repeat itself. A single act becomes an attitude, and then a habit, and then character is fixed. By a series of neglect, the individual has drifted far from the Good Shepherd and is lost! A professor once said, "I didn't intend to lose my religion; I just kept it in the drawer for safekeeping, but when I came back for it, it was gone."

Sometimes a person gets lost through the carelessness of someone else. Children may be lost because of the parents' neglect. Church members may be lost because of the pastor's neglect. Others are lost because of the neighbors' neglect. It is a solemn thought to realize that someone in my own home, my own church, or right next door may be lost because of my failure to pray or to witness for Christ.

Disobedience

How was the son lost? Not through carelessness, but willful disobedience. His father pleaded with him, his elder brother advised him, but he deliberately spurned their love and advice, packed up his suitcase, and left home. He took his own way and went into the far country—and there he got lost!

Many are lost spiritually because of their own free choice. They knew the difference between right and wrong; they could weigh the consequences of their action. Deliberately they chose their own way against God's way. They said in their hearts, "Not Thy will, but mine be done." But note this fact. Whether people are lost through mere carelessness or through willful disobedience, the result is one and the same. They are lost and away from the Father's home. Nothing is more pitiful; nothing more tragic.

This parable reveals not only the twofold path to sin but also the twofold *nature* of sin.

The Twofold Nature of Sin

Sins of the Flesh

The younger son stands for the sins of the flesh. He disobeyed his father and left home. He gave free rein to his physical passions and appetites. He wasted his substance in riotous living—in drunkenness, gambling, gluttony, and adultery. In the end he lost everything—his possessions, his friends, his reputation, his self-respect, and his decency. He ended up among the pigs. He had spurned home cooking; now he had to eat husks. He didn't want to obey his loving father; now he had to obey a cruel taskmaster. He wanted to be "free," but now he was a slave.

Some have ruined their lives by falling into the grosser sins of the flesh and wallowing in the mire of sin. They have become slaves to their animal appetites and passions. They have wasted their talents and opportunities and have lost their character and self-respect. They have wandered far from God and the Church; their lives are marred and ruined.

Sins of the Spirit

What about the elder son? He stands for the more subtle sins of the spirit. He didn't leave home and go into the far country. He didn't waste his substance in riotous living. He stayed right at home, labored faithfully, and saved his money. Outwardly he appeared to be a model son, in strong contrast to his wayward younger brother. But when the younger son returned home, the true character of this elder brother came to the surface. He was filled with jealousy because of the attention given to his brother; he was full of resentment and hatred; he was childish and peevish. He was physically close to his father, but spiritually far from him in heart and mind. He, too, was lost—right at home.

What is the picture we get at the end of the parable? We find the younger son, now restored to fellowship, on the inside of the home, feasting and rejoicing. But we see the elder son, resentful and angry, standing outside the house, refusing to go in. What a tragic scene!

Many people are like the elder brother. They wouldn't stoop to commit any of the grosser sins of the flesh, like drunkenness and immorality, but at the same time they are besieged with the more subtle sins of the spirit. They are jealous, resentful, full of anger. They are proud, self-righteous, and self-satisfied; they have no concern for others and no real love for God. And very often these people are much slower to realize their spiritual condition and turn to God in repentance than those who are living in outward sin and are far from the Kingdom.

Just remember: whether you are like the younger son or like the elder son, you are a prodigal just the same and need to repent and get right with God.

The Twofold Nature of Salvation

God's Part

The parable clearly teaches that in salvation God has a part and we have a part. It is God's part to seek and to save; it is our part to repent and return to the Father.

What did the shepherd do when he discovered the sheep was lost? He went out and looked for it until he found it. God is like that. He will undergo any hardship, make any sacrifice, to bring the lost back to the fold. What did the woman do when she discovered the coin was lost? She swept the whole house until she found it. Again, God is like that. He will sweep the whole universe to find a lost soul. He is seeking you today.

Do you fully grasp the significance of this glorious truth? It means that no person is ever more than one step away from God, for every time he or she takes a step in sin, God takes a step in love. God is always just one step behind, calling, pleading, inviting. So it is the easiest thing in the world for us to find God. All we have to do is to turn around—one short step—and we are in the arms of redeeming love! All we have to do is to be willing to be found.

Our Part

In the story of the prodigal son, we find the human aspect of salvation clearly emphasized. The father didn't go into the far country in search of his son. The son left of his own free choice; he must return of his own free will. It would do no good for the father to go out and take the son by the nape of the neck and drag him back home. He would be out of the far country, true, but the far country would still be in him. And so the father patiently waits, and in waiting he silently suffers, until the son returns home of his own accord.

In like manner we must realize our lost condition, turn our backs on the old life, return in penitence to the Heavenly Father, and confess our disobedience and waywardness. When we do that, then God will again do His part. He will give us the kiss of forgiveness, offer the ring of adoption, place upon us the robe of righteousness, and order the feast of rejoicing. God stands ever ready and eager to do His part. The only question is—are we ready to do ours?

Several years ago a young man quarreled with his father and in a fit of anger ran away from home. He journeyed to a distant city and there began to make his living. But after a few years a great desire arose in his heart to go back home. So he sat down and wrote to his father of his intention to return home. "Dear Dad," he wrote, "In a few days I will start for home. But one question constantly haunts me: Will you be angry with me and refuse to see me, or will you be willing to forgive and receive me? If you are willing to take me back, please put a yellow ribbon in the apple tree behind the house. If I see a ribbon there, I will get down from the train and come back home. If I don't see the ribbon, I will stay on the train."

After a few days he started on his journey. As the train got closer and closer to his hometown, the young man became more and more nervous. The thought uppermost in his mind was—will the ribbon be there? Will Dad receive me?

Now the train was pulling into the hometown. He could see the old farm from a distance. Soon the house came into view, and then the tree. Suddenly he jumped up from his seat with a shout: "Look! There's a yellow ribbon on every branch of that tree!"

God has strewn His yellow ribbons all over the world. Everywhere we look, we see evidence of His love and grace. Don't be afraid to turn to Him today, for He stands ready and willing to forgive and receive you. As He himself has said, "The one who comes to Me I will by no means cast out" (John 6:37). This is His personal promise to you today.

17

THE YOUNGER SON WHO LEFT HOME

Scripture passage: Reread Luke 15:11-24, included in the scripture passage at the beginning of chapter 16.

Key verse: "And he arose and came to his father" (v. 20).

The parable of the prodigal son is one of the most tender and moving stories that Jesus ever told. It is so human in its details. Take the framework of the story, localize it in any setting, and it would be true to the facts even in the 21st century. It is so human because it is related to the most human of all institutions—the family, the home. And yet the parable is so divine in its revelation. It so perfectly reveals the heart of the Heavenly Father, whose eyes scan the horizon and roam the entire earth, looking for the return of prodigal sons and daughters; and when they return, He is ready and eager to forgive and welcome them back home.

What are the spiritual lessons we learn from the story of the younger son?

He began with the wrong attitude. His downfall begins with the words "Give me." He did not say to his father, "How can I help you, Dad? How can I make my life useful?" or "I wonder what my father wants me to do." Like many youth of today, he was looking only for what he could get. Sin always begins in the attitude "*My* rights, *my* portion of goods." The essence of sin is to forget that *all* belongs to God, our Heavenly Father; to think that I am my own god. One great theologian defines sin as "the attempt of the creature to usurp the place and authority of the Creator." Instead of being a spoke revolving around the center, sin wants to become the hub itself.

He soon discovered the treacherous nature of sin. The boy thought there was glamor in the "far country." He felt he was going places, going to see things, going to have lots of fun. After all, Father was so old-fashioned, such a killjoy. Perhaps a traveler had come through and described the distant city to him. The boy's imagination had been aroused, and he began to dream about all its promised pleasures; and the more he dreamed, the more dull Father's house became. Yuck—those same old tables and chairs, those same windows to look out of, that same sofa, that same bed to sleep in. The far-off country of sin held out so many promises. So he left home.

At first it was wonderful—he was free! No one told him what to do. Mother didn't scold him when his room was untidy. Father didn't call him to work. He had so many friends. All the guys laughed at his jokes. All the girls told him he was very handsome (as long as his money lasted). "But when he had spent all, there arose a severe famine in the land, and he began to be in want." It always happens that way: at the end of every sin is a famine, a hunger, a deep dissatisfaction—for sin is a liar. It can make promises, but it cannot fulfill them. Why? Because it doesn't make any difference as to how much enjoyment and stimulation you have; when your heart is made for *home* and you are away from *home,* you cannot be permanently happy. Sin is deceptive, treacherous. It promises much but delivers misery and unhappiness. It promises the glitter of a "far country" but produces the garbage of a pigsty.

He awakened and came to himself. How? He remembered Father and home! Suddenly it dawned upon him: he was meant to be a *son,* not a *pig;* he was human, not an animal. Ah, just as the eye is made for light, the ear for sound, a violin for the master's touch, so our souls are made for Jesus Christ. Nothing less than Christ can permanently satisfy. God has stamped upon us an indelible image, a memory of home and what we are meant to be—sons and daughters of God—and we can never get away from this.

One day an accident occurred on a highway. The driver was killed, but the life of his young son was spared. When the boy saw his father's dead body lying in the ditch, he began to cry profusely. Several drivers stopped to help. One man pulled out a $10 bill and handed it to the boy and said, "Sonny, don't cry. Take this money, and buy yourself something." Through his tears the lad cried out, "I want my daddy! I want my daddy!" Someone else offered him some candy, another person a ticket to the ball game. But each time the boy cried out, "I want my daddy! I want my daddy!" Nothing else would satisfy him. Likewise, something in the human heart cries out, "I want my Heavenly Father!" and nothing else can satisfy.

The young man's whole attitude changed. In the beginning he had said, "Give me"; now he is changed and says, *"Make* me!" Now he is not interested in what *he wants,* but what his *father wills.* "I'm not worthy . . . make me a servant," he prepares to say. Everyone who repents has this about-face attitude; it is a godly sorrow that brings with it a determination to be made different. This shows the human element in our salvation and makes this parable different from that of the lost sheep and lost coin. In their case, the sheep and coin did nothing to be found, but in the case of the lost son, he had to *arise and go.* He had to decide for himself to go home. We cannot save ourselves—never! But we must be willing to forsake sin; we must be willing to be changed. God does all the seeking and the saving, but we alone can make the response.

He sees the true nature of his father. He had discovered the true nature of sin, its treachery and deceit. Now he discovers the true nature of his father. What a beautiful picture of our Heavenly Father, who sees us a long way off and comes running to meet us at a great distance. They say "love is blind." Not so with God's love—it is far-sighted! And what does the father in the story do? Does he say, "Aha—that rascal of a son! He's spent his money; now he comes back in rags and expects me to take him back? I'll have to teach him a lesson!"

No, no. Here is God in all His forgiving, self-forgetting love. But even this parable is not the final, New Testament picture of God, for it was told before the event of the Cross. Now we see an even greater truth. Now we know that the Holy Spirit himself was with the younger son, right in the middle of the pigsty. It was He who talked to the boy there and brought him to his senses; it was He who reminded the boy of home. For the Cross and the coming of the Holy Spirit show us that the Father not only comes running to meet us halfway but has *gone all the way to save us.* Oh, the matchless love of the Father! His is the "love that will not let me go."

18

THE ELDER SON WHO STAYED AT HOME

Scripture passage: Luke 15:25-32

> Now his older son was in the field. And as he came and drew near to the house, he heard music and dancing. So he called one of the servants and asked what these things meant. And he said to him, "Your brother has come, and because he has received him safe and sound, your father has killed the fatted calf."
>
> And he was angry and would not go in. Therefore his father came out and pleaded with him. So he answered and said to his father, "Lo, these many years I have been serving you; I never transgressed your commandment at any time; and yet you never gave me a young goat, that I might make merry with my friends. But as soon as this son of yours came, who has devoured your livelihood with harlots, you killed the fatted calf for him."
>
> And he said to him, "Son, you are always with me, and all that I have is yours. It was right that we should make merry and be glad, for your brother was dead and is alive again, and was lost and is found."

Key verse: "Son, you are always with me, and all that I have is yours" (v. 31).

We usually call this story the parable of the prodigal *son,* but in truth it is the parable of the prodigal *sons.* Both boys were prodigal. The younger brother was a prodigal who went into *a far country;* the elder brother was a prodigal who stayed *at home.* One was prodigal of his father's *substance* with *riotous living;* the other was prodigal of his father's *love* with *respectable living.*

Both brothers were sinners. One sinned in the *flesh;* the other

103

sinned in the *spirit*. One sinned in his *actions;* the other sinned in his *reactions*. One was a sinner in his *outer deportment;* the other in his *inner disposition*. One was guilty of the sins of *commission;* the other the sins of *omission*.

When we hear this story, we don't usually think much about the elder brother. This is regrettable, for he is one of the chief characters of the whole parable. The main point that Jesus was trying to drive home to the Pharisees on that day was that they were so much like the elder son—religious and strict, but out of fellowship with the Father. They were unforgiving and unloving, proud and censorious.

Perhaps we intentionally forget the elder brother, because we are too much like him ourselves. We see the reflection of our own character in his portrait. But it is good for us to take a long, close look at this elder brother.

Let us look at the tragedy of his *thoughts* that led to the tragedy of his *life*.

The elder son was mistaken about his relationship. He thought of his relationship to his father in terms of *physical contact*, not *spiritual communion*. He thought because he stayed at home, ate at his father's table, and worked in his father's field that he was in right relationship to his father. But a correct relationship to the father consists of kinship of mind, oneness of heart. This is not a matter of geographical proximity, but of spiritual companionship.

Some people think that because they are members of Christian homes or members of a church, they are members of the kingdom of God. Far from it! It is possible to be *in* a church but *out* of the Kingdom. It is possible to eat at the Father's table—to partake of the bread and wine at a Communion service—and yet be spiritually starved within. It is possible for the body to be in the Father's house, but the mind and heart to be in the far country.

The elder brother thought of himself as a *servant*, not as a *son*. Notice what he said to his father: "Lo, these many years I have been serving you; I never transgressed your commandment at any time; and yet you never gave me a young goat, that I might make merry with my friends." These are indignant, self-righteous words—strange language for a son, fit language for a servant.

The elder brother was a hard worker but a heartless son. God is more interested in good sons than in hard workers. We cannot substitute service for goodness. It is possible to be a hard worker—to sing in the choir, serve on committees, even be in full-time Christian service —and yet not be a good son or daughter. Of course, if we are good sons or daughters, we will be good workers as well, for being children of God does not exempt us from service.

The elder brother served out of a sense of *duty,* not out of a spirit of *love.* Servants obey and serve because they *have to;* sons obey and serve because they *want to.*

The elder son also thought that relationship was a one-way connection. He thought he could be in right relationship with his father without being in right relationship with his brother. But relationship is a two-way connection. It is both vertical and horizontal. We can't be out of fellowship with our fellow human beings and maintain our fellowship with God.

The elder son was mistaken about the true nature of righteousness. Righteousness is more than just a matter of correct actions; it is also a matter of *Christlike reactions.*

The younger brother sinned in his *actions.* His was the sin of loose living, so loose, in fact, that life fell to pieces. Sin has no cement to hold life together. Sin blasts and destroys. But the younger son came back to his father's house and confessed his sin and folly. He was forgiven and restored to fellowship. His father invited guests, and they had a big party.

The elder brother sinned in his *reactions.* As he came back from the field that evening, he heard music and dancing. He called one of the servants and asked him, "What does this mean?" The servant replied, "Sir, your younger brother returned about noon today, and your father is beside himself with joy. He hired a local combo and ordered us to make a feast." When the elder son heard this, his face hardened. So what did he do?

He reacted with *self-righteousness.* He said to his father, "All these years I have served you. I never broke a commandment." He compared himself with his renegade brother, and he looked great in comparison. But what a poor showing he made in front of his father!

He reacted with *resentment.* He would not even speak about the younger son as "my brother." Instead, he referred to him as "your son." Isn't it a good thing that when the younger brother returned home, he first met his father? What if he had met his older brother first? He probably would have headed straight back to the pigsty.

The elder brother reacted with *jealousy.* "You kill for him—this useless son of yours—the fatted calf." He reacted with *self-pity*. "You never gave *me* a party!"

He reacted also with *anger*. The record states that he was angry and refused to go into the house. So when the curtain falls on this drama, the younger son, who sinned but repented, was on the inside rejoicing, while the elder son, who sinned in his reactions and did not repent, was on the outside alone.

Do unholy reactions and attitudes keep us from fellowship with the Heavenly Father? They certainly do! What happens to you when someone sins against you? Do you react with anger, sullen hate, fear, resentment, bitterness? That is one test of being a Christian.

Righteousness is more than something negative—just refraining from doing certain things. Righteousness is something positive. The elder son thought that because he did not break his father's *commandments,* he was righteous. But at the same time he was breaking his father's *heart* by his unconcern, unforgiving spirit, and lack of love. True righteousness is not something put *on;* it is put *in* by the grace of God.

The elder son was mistaken about his responsibility. He thought that if he was faithful in the field—if he plowed, sowed seed, spread fertilizer, then harvested the crop—his father would be satisfied. But he failed miserably in his responsibility to his younger brother. He had no concern, no love, no forgiveness.

Right here is one of the main points of the parable. Jesus was saying to the Pharisees that day, "You are concerned about lost sheep and lost coins, but not about lost sons and daughters. If a sheep gets lost, you will search the whole hillside until you find it. If a coin gets lost, you'll push aside all the furniture and sweep the whole house until you find it. But if sons or daughters of Israel are lost, you do nothing to restore them to the fold. In fact, when a repentant child comes back home, you grumble and criticize."

God is primarily interested in seeking lost people, and He wants us to be concerned also. This is the sign of being a good son or daughter, the sign of a right relationship with the Father. When we are born of God, we receive the nature of God and become interested in what He is interested in and involved in what He is involved in.

I remember listening to a missionary doctor in India presenting a Bible study on the parable of the prodigal son. He added something to the story that I believe is in full accord with the Spirit of Christ. He said that when the younger son came back home and was restored to full fellowship, he began working in the father's field once again and was subject to his discipline. Then one day he said to his father, "Dad, I've decided to go back to the far country for a while. Please give me your permission."

His father's face turned sad. "Please don't mention it, son. You have already broken your mother's and my heart once. Don't do it again."

"Don't worry, Dad," he replied with a smile. "I'm going for an entirely different reason this time. You see—while I was there, I met a lot of prodigal sons and daughters. I want to tell them that if they return home, Father will be there to welcome and forgive them."

This is the main responsibility of the children of God—to remind the lost that the Heavenly Father is waiting for them to come back home.

The elder son was mistaken about his resources. Observe the force of this dialogue between the father and his elder son. The son said, "Lo, these many years I have been serving you . . . yet you never gave me a young goat, that I might make merry with my friends." The father replied, "Son, you are always with me, and all that I have is yours!" The elder son was fabulously rich and didn't know it. He was living far below his resources. He didn't have because he didn't ask. He could have been feasting all the time, but he never claimed his possessions.

Many Christians are living far below their spiritual resources and privileges. They are without joy, when God offers them "joy unspeakable and full of glory." They are without peace, when God wants them to have "peace . . . which passeth all understanding [and misunderstanding too]" (Phil. 4:7, KJV). They are defeated and discouraged when God wants them to be "more than conquerors" (Rom. 8:37) through Christ, the all-victorious One. They are fruitless and ineffective, when God wants to endue them with "power from on high" (Luke 24:49) so that they will bear much fruit.

A few years ago in Hollywood, Florida, an elderly woman suddenly died. Her husband had been a lawyer in New England, and upon his death she had moved to Florida. She dressed shabbily and lived alone in an old, ramshackle house. In sympathy the neighbors picked her up in their cars and took her to the supermarkets or out for an evening drive. Once a week a maid came and helped her clean house. One day when the maid entered the house, she found the lady dead in her bed.

The maid immediately informed the police, and while they were inspecting the house, they found approximately a million dollars in currency, stuffed away in old shoeboxes and cartons. Upon further investigation, they discovered that she had a savings account in the bank with almost another million dollars. Since the widow's death was sudden, an autopsy was ordered by the police. Imagine the surprise of all when the diagnosis was made known: malnutrition! Think of it—she was a millionaire but was living like a pauper.

Isn't this a picture of many people today? They are potentially rich in Christ but are living like spiritual beggars, simply because they have not claimed their total inheritance in Christ.

So in looking into the mirror of God's Word, have you seen yourself? In looking at the elder brother, have you seen the reflection of your own character?

Are you in relationship with your Heavenly Father? If not, you need to enter into fellowship with Him and become His son or daughter.

Have you been depending upon your own self-righteousness and good deeds rather than receiving in humility God's true righteousness? Remember: true goodness is found in Him.

Have you failed in your responsibility to others? Have you been more interested in your own welfare and progress than in the needs and welfare of those around you? If so, then repent of your unconcern and carelessness, and surrender yourself to a life of service and helpfulness.

Have you been living far below your potential resources, seeking to face life and its problems in your own strength and wisdom? If so, then avail yourself of all the divine resources that God is offering you, and go out to live radiantly and victoriously. The Heavenly Father is saying to you, "Son, daughter, all I have is yours for the asking!"

19

THE PHARISEE AND THE TAX COLLECTOR

Scripture passage: Luke 18:9-14

> He spoke this parable to some who trusted in themselves that they were righteous, and despised others: "Two men went up to the temple to pray, one a Pharisee and the other a tax collector. "The Pharisee stood and prayed thus with himself, 'God, I thank You that I am not like other men—extortioners, unjust, adulterers, or even as this tax collector. I fast twice a week; I give tithes of all that I possess.'
>
> "And the tax collector, standing afar off, would not so much as raise his eyes to heaven, but beat his breast, saying, 'God, be merciful to me a sinner!'
>
> "I tell you, this man went down to his house justified rather than the other; for everyone who exalts himself will be abased, and he who humbles himself will be exalted."

Key verse: "This man went down to his house justified rather than the other" (v. 14).

Many of the parables Jesus told were based on a striking contrast between two different individuals. For example, in the parable of the Good Samaritan, we see the contrast between the priest who passed by and the Samaritan who stopped to help. In Jesus' parable about Lazarus and the rich man, we find the contrast is between the selfish rich man who went to hell and the pitiful beggar, Lazarus, who went to heaven. In the parable of the prodigal son, we note the contrast is between the younger son, who went into a far country, and the elder son, who stayed at home. And now, in this parable, we see the contrast between a self-righteous Pharisee and a penitent tax collector.

Two men. Luke, the Gospel writer, states clearly that Jesus told this parable to "some who trusted in themselves that they were righteous, and despised others." So Jesus is dealing with real characters, not just caricatures. We cannot read this story without automatically identifying ourselves with one or the other of the two men.

Jesus said, "Two men went up to the temple to pray." One was a Pharisee, who represented the religious elite of Jesus' day. The Pharisees were a lay-oriented sect of teachers and interpreters of the Law. They held distinctive doctrines such as a belief in angels, immortality of the soul, resurrection of the dead, and divine control of history, but doubtless their most distinguishing characteristic was concern for the Law.

The Pharisees gave themselves to knowing and interpreting the Law. Their interpretations, transmitted orally as "the tradition of the elders," were considered to be as binding as, if not more so than, the written Law. Such concern for the Law came from a practical, sincere desire to keep the Law, since the Pharisees believed that one's standing before God was determined by strict adherence to the Law. This religion of merit based on works led to a sense of self-righteousness and to a lifestyle of rigorous legalism and separation from the rest of society.

The other man was a "publican" (tax collector), who represented a socially despised group in Jesus' day. The publicans were members of a company to which the Romans auctioned off the right to collect taxes. They were required to give security for the amount the government should receive. They sold to others certain portions of the revenue. Publicans were engaged to do the actual collection of the customs and were notorious for their crookedness and extortion. A Jewish publican was a social outcast, looked upon with contempt because he raised taxes for a foreign and heathen government.

These two men—Pharisee and publican—went to the same place, the Temple, for the same reason: to pray. We can certainly commend both of them for their good intention. Prayer is one of the most important duties and privileges in the spiritual life of any person. As air is to the lungs, so is prayer to the soul. Jesus taught His disciples how to pray and exhorted them to "always . . . pray and not lose heart" (Luke 18:1). Paul exhorts us to "pray without ceasing" (1 Thess. 5:17). In fact, nearly every religion gives prominence to the practice of prayer.

So far so good. Both men had good intentions. They went to a good place, the Temple. They were engaged in a good exercise, prayer.

The difference becomes obvious when we note the content of their prayers and the spirit in which they prayed.

Two prayers. It is very possible to do a good deed with the wrong motive and in a wrong spirit. A person may give generously to charity just to receive the applause of the public. One may fast and pray just to appear deeply spiritual to others. A pastor may seek to preach a good sermon in order to receive the acclaim of listeners. A person may go to church just to improve business in the community.

Look at the prayer of the Pharisee. The parable says that "he prayed thus with himself." True prayer is always offered to God and Him alone, but the Pharisee was more or less just talking to himself. He was really giving himself a testimonial before God. His was a self-righteous prayer. First, he compared himself to others, especially with the publican. He said, "God, I thank You that I am not like other men —extortioners, unjust, adulterers, or even as this tax collector." Then he began to boast of his own good deeds. "I fast twice a week; I give tithes of all that I possess." And in the presence of the tax collector, he looked like a very moral and upright individual, one to be respected and modeled. But in the presence of God he showed up as a hypocrite and a sinner. The big question of life is not "How do I stack up with my fellow human beings?" but "How do I appear before God?"

The main defect in the Pharisee's prayer was that he dared to approach God on the basis of his own goodness rather than the grace of God himself. Human goodness is like filthy rags in the sight of God (see Isa. 64:6). Apart from the grace of God, we have no right to enter into His presence.

In contrast, consider the prayer offered by the publican. He prayed in the spirit of humility and contrition. The parable tells us that "standing afar off, [he] would not so much as raise his eyes to heaven, but beat his breast." Perhaps when he entered the Temple, the house of God, he became so aware of the presence of the holy God that in comparison he immediately saw his sinfulness and unworthiness. So he hung his head in shame.

Now the publican could have easily turned the tables on the Pharisee. He might have compared himself with him and said something like "God, I know at times I have been deceptive and selfish in the tax-collecting business, but I thank You that I am not like this proud, self-righteous Pharisee. He's nothing but a hypocrite. At least I'm open and honest about myself."

A Sunday School teacher presented a very moving lesson on this parable to her class of young people. When she finished her exposition, she said solemnly to the class, "And now, children, let us bow our heads in prayer and thank God that we are not like that nasty old Pharisee!" It is so easy to fall into the pharasaical pit.

But the publican humbled himself and cast himself solely on the mercy, the grace, of God. He prayed in all sincerity, "God, be merciful to me a sinner!" It was one of the simplest and shortest prayers that any person could offer his Creator.

Two results. Jesus concluded the parable by saying, "I tell you, this man went down to his house justified rather than the other." The publican found forgiveness for his sins and went home a new person. Most likely he ceased his crooked and deceitful ways and became an honest tax collector from then on. This most certainly would have surprised all his clients! We can say this with a high degree of assurance when we remember the story of another tax collector in real life, Zacchaeus, and the transformation that took place in his life when he met Jesus.

As for the Pharisee, he went home unjustified, unforgiven, the same old person, knowing only a form of righteousness without experiencing its power.

What about *your* prayers? Do you offer them in the right spirit, with the right motive? Do you approach God on the basis of your own goodness or on the basis of His grace? Does your praying leave you in your former condition, or does it change you into the person God wants you to be?

20

DIVES AND LAZARUS

Scripture passage: Luke 16:19-31

There was a certain rich man who was clothed in purple and fine linen and fared sumptuously every day. But there was a certain beggar named Lazarus, full of sores, who was laid at his gate, desiring to be fed with the crumbs which fell from the rich man's table. Moreover the dogs came and licked his sores.

So it was that the beggar died, and was carried by the angels to Abraham's bosom. The rich man also died and was buried. And being in torments in Hades, he lifted up his eyes and saw Abraham afar off, and Lazarus in his bosom. Then he cried and said, "Father Abraham, have mercy on me, and send Lazarus that he may dip the tip of his finger in water and cool my tongue; for I am tormented in this flame."

But Abraham said, "Son, remember that in your lifetime you received your good things, and likewise Lazarus evil things; but now he is comforted and you are tormented. And besides all this, between us and you there is a great gulf fixed, so that those who want to pass from here to you cannot, nor can those from there pass to us."

Then he said, "I beg you therefore, father, that you would send him to my father's house, for I have five brothers, that he may testify to them, lest they also come to this place of torment."

Abraham said to him, "They have Moses and the prophets; let them hear them."

And he said, "No, father Abraham; but if one goes to them from the dead, they will repent."

But he said to him, "If they do not hear Moses and the prophets, neither will they be persuaded though one rise from the dead."

Key verse: "If they do not hear Moses and the prophets, neither will they be persuaded though one rise from the dead" (v. 31).

In this parable Jesus pulls back the curtain and gives us a brief glimpse of life after death. The parable is a drama in two acts—the first being enacted here on earth, the second in the life to come.

Act One—Life on Earth

We find two contrasting actors in this drama. First is the rich man, who is usually called "Dives," the Latin word for "rich." Second is the poor beggar named "Lazarus," which is the Latin form of "Eleazer," meaning "God is my help."

Dives lived in the lap of luxury. The parable tells us that he was "clothed in purple and fine linen and fared sumptuously every day." No doubt this brief description of his apparel and food is merely indicative of other forms of wealth that he enjoyed, such as a luxurious home with a retinue of servants, and an array of comforts and conveniences. Dives himself is a picture of indolence and self-indulgence.

Here is Lazarus, a miserable beggar, who camped just outside the gate of Dives's estate. The only food he had was "the crumbs which fell from the rich man's table." He lived on garbage and leftovers. Moreover, his body was full of sores, and the only comfort he gained was from the neighborhood dogs that licked his open wounds. Lazarus is a picture of helpless and abject poverty. Thus, while Dives wallowed in luxury, Lazarus suffered in hunger and pain.

According to the parable, in due time both men died. We can only imagine how the people responded to the two events. When Lazarus died, people turned their faces away from the horrible bundle of rags at the gate. Nobody had a funeral for him; his body was probably thrown out on the city dump and burned. But Jesus tells us that "he was carried by the angels to Abraham's bosom," that is, to heaven. As for Dives, when he died, there was probably a large gathering of relatives and friends, with many complimentary eulogies, much pomp and ceremony, and a large procession to the cemetery. But Dives landed in hell.

We must not think that Lazarus went to heaven just because he was poor and that Dives went to hell simply because he was rich. Though the parable does not tell us in so many words, on the basis of other scripture we can infer that Lazarus must have been a man of faith and love for God. For the only way anyone enters the Kingdom is by the grace of God through faith. Perhaps Lazarus spent many pain-filled, lonely hours in prayer.

Dives did not go to hell just because he was rich. Wealth is not evil in itself—only the misuse of wealth. Wealth is neutral in character. It can be a means of selfishness and evil; it can also be an instrument of generosity and great good. We can use our possessions for our own comfort and enjoyment, or we can use them for the glory of God and benefit of others. Wealth can be dangerous, but it can also be highly beneficial.

What was the sin of Dives? He didn't order his guards to remove Lazarus from the gate. He didn't curse him whenever he saw him. Rather, his was the sin of omission, the sin of indifference. He must have seen Lazarus whenever he went out anywhere, but he never took real notice of him and showed no compassion for him. In short, he simply *did nothing.* He looked at a fellow human being, hungry and in pain, and did nothing about it.

Act Two—Life After Death

Scene 1: Lazarus is described as "in Abraham's bosom" and being "comforted." This is a picturesque way of describing the close fellowship, love, and sense of security and belonging that Lazarus enjoyed in heaven. These are all parts of a wholesome life.

In contrast, Dives is pictured as being "tormented," to such an extent that he cries out to Abraham in anguish and pleads with him to send Lazarus to "dip the tip of his finger in water and cool my tongue."

Just think of all the times on earth that Lazarus had begged Dives for some food to eat or some ointment to soothe his sores, and Dives paid no attention, but passed by in utter disdain. Now Dives begs for the same Lazarus to come and minister to him in his torment.

What were the component parts of the torment that Dives experienced?

First—*memory.* In response to Dives's plea for mercy, Abraham said to him, "Son, *remember* that in your lifetime you received your good things, and likewise Lazarus evil things; but now he is comforted and you are tormented" (emphasis added).

Now Dives's memory was sharpened, quickened. He could never forget his selfishness, self-indulgence, indifference, lack of compassion, and arrogance. There was nothing to help him forget—-no television set, radio, football games, movies, tranquilizers, or liquor to soothe or blur his memory. All his false security—money, position, authority, and comfort—were gone. His memory was like a continuous this-is-your-life television show that passed before his eyes and reminded him day and night of all his past failures and sins. God's grace through Calvary takes the sting out of memory to the forgiven; memory is buried in the depths of God's love. Heaven will be blessed by memory. But hell? It will be blighted by memory.

Second—*self-consciousness*. In hell Dives found true self-knowledge. He stood naked before himself and God and saw himself as he really was. He was compelled to see what he never believed. His selfishness was bared. He loved himself and took care of himself; now he was *all alone* by himself.

In his book *The Great Divorce*, C. S. Lewis pictures hell as a place of isolation. The people in hell just can't stand one another; they continuously get on one another's nerves. They keep moving farther and farther away from each other. So there are no friends or neighbors in hell. Everybody is all alone.

Third—*separation*. When Dives asked Abraham to send Lazarus with a drop of water to cool his tongue, Abraham answered, "Between us and you there is a great gulf fixed, so that those who want to pass from here to you cannot, nor can those who want to come from there pass to us." Here we see the very essence of hell—eternal separation from God, the finality of decision, the fixation of character. Even though Dives could now see and know the truth, he could do nothing about it. The time to repent and receive God's grace had passed. The time of mercy had passed. Hell is a place where God is not. He can no longer reach the sinner there; the sinner can no longer reach Him.

Who dug this spiritual Grand Canyon? God? No, Dives himself. He could have built bridges with his wealth, but instead, he dug an impassable chasm. The sinner digs a great ditch spoonful by spoonful, spadeful by spadeful, shovelful by shovelful, bulldozerful by bulldozerful.

Dives was remorseful but not repentant. In hell the capacity for remorse is retained, but there is no capacity for repentance, no possibility of change. Oh, the eternal fixedness of it all!

C. S. Lewis suggests that in the final analysis there are only two groups of people in the world. First are those who say to God, "Not my will, but Thine be done." Jesus was the great example of this group when He prayed this very prayer in the Garden of Gethsemane. God eventually has to say to the second group, "Not My will, but thine be done." And C. S. Lewis suggests that when God has to say to a person, "You didn't want My will for your life; all right—you can have your will, and you can have it forever," *that is hell!*

Scene 2: In this scene, Dives makes a second request: "I beg you therefore, father, that you would send him to my father's house, for I have five brothers, that he may testify to them, lest they also come to this place of torment."

This is the first unselfish thought that Dives entertained. For once he actually thought of someone other than himself. It's interesting that he was in hell only a short time and suddenly became mission-minded. "Send someone to my brothers," he pleaded. But at the heart of his request was a subtle inference. What he was really saying was, "Abraham, I really never had a chance; at least give my brothers a chance."

Abraham answered, "They have Moses and the prophets; let them hear them."

And Dives replied, "No, father Abraham; but if one goes to them from the dead, they will repent."

Abraham said, "If they do not hear Moses and the prophets, neither will they be persuaded though one rise from the dead."

Herein lies the main point of the parable. Jesus was saying to His listeners that it's not how much light or truth people have that counts, but how they respond to whatever light they already have. Unless people walk in the light they already know, they will not accept further light when it comes.

When another man named Lazarus, brother of Mary and Martha, was raised from the dead, did the Jewish leaders believe? No—they sought to kill him. When Jesus was raised from the dead, did they believe? No—they tried to kill the apostles who preached the Resurrection. If you don't have an ear for the prophets, you won't have an eye for the Resurrection. If you won't listen to the moral Law, you won't believe the miracle. If you don't obey what you have, the little things, it's doubtful that you would obey the big dramatic things.

What if Jesus would come today and rise from the dead, would you believe? Are you waiting for something spectacular, while you are not accepting the little evidences and truths? God will not perform a miracle so great that He will overcome your decision. He is not a shock therapist, working on your nerves. He's a loving Father working on your heart.

What do you have to do now to get right with God? Be true to the little light you have or you will be blinded by the greater light when it comes. Begin with the obvious wrong in your life and set it right. Go from there. We all have enough light to start on.

21

THE SOWER, THE SEED, AND THE SOILS

Scripture passage: Matt. 13:1-9; 18-23

On the same day Jesus went out of the house and sat by the sea. And great multitudes were gathered together to Him, so that He got into a boat and sat; and the whole multitude stood on the shore. Then He spoke many things to them in parables, saying: "Behold, a sower went out to sow. And as he sowed, some seed fell by the wayside; and the birds came and devoured them. Some fell on stony places, where they did not have much earth; and they immediately sprang up because they had no depth of earth. But when the sun was up they were scorched, and because they had no root they withered away. And some fell among thorns, and the thorns sprang up and choked them. But others fell on good ground and yielded a crop: some a hundredfold, some sixty, some thirty. He who has ears to hear, let him hear!" . . .

"Therefore hear the parable of the sower: When anyone hears the word of the kingdom, and does not understand it, then the wicked one comes and snatches away what was sown in his heart. This is he who received seed by the wayside. But he who received the seed on stony places, this is he who hears the word and immediately receives it with joy; yet he has no root in himself, but endures only for a while. For when tribulation or persecution arises because of the word, immediately he stumbles. Now he who received seed among the thorns is he who hears the word, and the cares of this world and the deceitfulness of riches choke the word, and he becomes unfruitful. But he who received seed on the good ground is he who hears the word and understands it, who indeed bears fruit and produces: some a hundredfold, some sixty, some thirty."

Key verse: "A sower went out to sow" (v. 3).

As Jesus went about the countryside preaching the good news of the kingdom of God, people responded to His message in different ways. Some were resistant, others receptive. Some listened superficially, others wholeheartedly. So Jesus told the parable of the sower both as a warning and as an encouragement—a warning to those who hear the message but don't practice it, and an encouragement to those who proclaim the message and at times don't see any results.

The Seed

Jesus said that the seed that was sown is the Word of God. He had confidence in the seed. He said on one occasion, "Heaven and earth will pass away, but My words will by no means pass away" (Matt. 24:35). The seed of the Word is good seed. If it fails to sprout and bear fruit, it's not the quality of the seed, but the quality of the soil that's at fault.

What is significant about seed? First, *a seed proceeds from life*. Whether it's as small as a mustard seed or as large as the acorn, a seed comes from prior, antecedent life. So it is with the Word of God as found in the Scriptures. It's alive with truth because it comes from life. Actually it comes from a *living person*—persons, yes, but ultimately from the Person of Jesus Christ. "All Scripture is God-breathed," we read in 2 Tim. 3:16 (NIV). Human beings were merely the instruments in bringing the Bible to birth. Life comes out of the Word, because life has gone into it.

A seed possesses life. It may appear inert, with no pulse, no action, no thought, but residing in it is the mystery of life. In the same way, the Bible, like any other book, is made up of ink, paper, glue, and binding, but God has put something into this Book that makes it different from all others. The Bible has boundless, deathless vitality. You don't have to defend the Bible. As Spurgeon, well-known 19th-century British Baptist preacher, said, "You might as well try to defend a lion. Just turn it loose."

The Word of God has *inherent life*. "Inherent" means "existing in; belonging to," not tacked on like tinsel onto a Christmas tree. The Bible is not subject to amendment like the Constitution of the United States.

The Word of God has *indestructible life*. Persistently and perversely, men and women have tried to get rid of the Bible, but no one has ever succeeded, and no one will. The Bible belongs to all lands, all times, and all ages.

A seed not only *proceeds* from life and *possesses* life but also *produces* life. It's creative. Plant the seed, and the earth, sun, and rain all combine to generate life and produce a harvest. Likewise, the vitality of God's Word is such that when it's proclaimed, instantly results begin to take place.

The Soils

There is one quality of seed, the Word of God, but there are different kinds of soil that determine the fortune of the seed.

First is *wayside soil*, trampled by people and beasts. The seed that falls on such a surface is unable to germinate. Birds of the air swoop down and devour it. Some hearers of the Word are so hardened by hostility or indifference that no message can find entrance into their hearts. No sooner has the truth been preached in their hearing than Satan comes and snatches it away.

Second is *rocky soil*, with a thin layer of earth over a shelf of limestone. The soil is good, but it lacks depth. The seed sprouts all right, but because of shallow roots the plant quickly withers under the blighting sun. Likewise, some readily accept the Word of God; their emotions are easily stirred. But they lack depth of conviction and, because of their superficial commitment, soon fall away when difficulties come.

Third is *thorny soil*. The seed takes root and springs up with promise, but thorns grow and choke the plant so that it cannot bear fruit. Some people gladly accept the Word and begin the Christian life, but in time they're overcome by the cares and pleasures of life so that they turn away from the truth.

Finally, we have *good soil*, which bears fruit, possibly thirtyfold, sixtyfold, even a hundredfold. By this figure our Lord described the true hearers who not only receive the Word but also continue to practice it in spite of opposition and difficulties and who influence the thinking of others by their righteous lives.

Thus with unforgettable vividness, the parable of the sower brings a warning to those who hear the gospel. There are different ways of hearing the Word of God, and the fruit that it produces depends on the mind-set of the one who accepts it.

Hearing is important. Jesus said, "He who has ears to hear, let him hear!" (Matt. 13:9). But hearing means more than just listening with our ears. It signifies spiritual perception and understanding.

The four different soils symbolize four degrees of hearing. The *wayside soil* stands for a *closed mind*, hardened by prejudice, pride, an unteachable spirit, self-centeredness, or fear of the truth. The Word of God has not the slightest chance of gaining entry into such a person's heart.

The *rocky soil* symbolizes the *casual mind*—gushy, emotional, impulsive, shallow. It receives the Word for a while but fails to retain it.

The *thorny soil* illustrates the *confused mind,* divided between ir-reconcilable loyalties. In the beginning some growth and prospects of fruit occur, but conflict arises, killing productivity.

The *good soil* is the *committed mind*—open, receptive, obedient, and persevering.

Hearing without doing is impertinent. It means that we're only playing with the truth; we are being frivolous—we don't mean busi-ness. Hearing converted into doing is *imperative*. It is necessary in or-der to build a solid foundation for our character. At the conclusion of His Sermon on the Mount, Jesus said, "Whoever hears these words of Mine, and does them, I will liken him to a wise man who built his house on the rock. . . . But everyone who hears these sayings of Mine, and does not do them, will be like a foolish man who built his house on the sand" (7:24, 26).

People do not by nature resemble one of these types of soil. They become like hard or rocky or thorny soil by their own choice. It's pos-sible for every person to be like the good soil.

The Harvest

The parable of the sower is not only a warning to those who hear the gospel but also an encouragement to those who proclaim the gospel. As messengers of the Word—whether we're pastors, missionar-ies, evangelists, Sunday School teachers, or simply one person witness-ing to another—we can have confidence in the seed of God's Word. There *will* be fruit; the harvest is sure. God's Word will not return void.

Tony Isip was a wealthy builder and land developer in Manila, cap-ital of the Philippines. He owned three beautiful mansions and had everything money could buy, but he was not happy. So he came home one afternoon with a loaded revolver in his pocket, determined to end his life. Then he noticed a package in the day's mail. When he opened it, he found a copy of the New Testament. Setting the revolver aside for a moment, he began reading. Soon he was so caught up with the message of Jesus in the Gospel of John that he forgot all about the gun. He read all night and the next day surrendered himself to the Lord.

During the next week, Tony went to every bookstore in Manila and bought all the Bibles he could find—10,000 copies. He began giving them away to friends, business partners, and anyone who would accept one. Then he started a Bible reading group in his own home. The group grew so large that he had to move it to the Intercontinental Hotel ballroom. Within four years, Tony had led more than 500 people to Christ, among them the manager of the hotel.

If you receive Christ, tell others about Him. When you do this, you're sowing the good seed of the gospel, and be assured: the harvest is sure. The psalmist writes, "Those who sow in tears shall reap in joy. He who continually goes forth weeping, bearing seed for sowing, shall doubtless come again with rejoicing, bringing his sheaves with him" (Ps. 126:5-6).

PART 3

The Miracles of Jesus

Jesus *said* certain things that we call *parables;* He *did* certain things that we call *miracles.* Jesus took truth and *spoke* it out in parables; He took truth and *acted* it out in miracles.

The people in Jesus' day reacted in the same way to His works as they did to His teachings. Mark writes in his Gospel, "They were *astonished* at His teaching, for He taught them as one having authority, and not as the scribes" (Mark 1:22, emphasis added). Then a few verses later he writes, "They were all *amazed* . . . saying . . . 'with authority He commands even the unclean spirits, and they obey Him'" (v. 27, emphasis added).

The miracles Jesus performed were a strong witness to His divinity and supernatural power. Jesus himself said to the people, "If I do not do the works of My Father, do not believe Me; but if I do, though you do not believe Me, believe the works, that you may know and believe that the Father is in Me, and I in Him" (John 10:37-38). It is true that the prophets of the Old Testament and the disciples in the New Testament also performed amazing miracles, but theirs was a *delegated* authority. Jesus performed miracles in His own *inherent* authority. As the Son of God, He had power to heal the sick, cast out demons, calm the stormy sea, and raise the dead.

Just as sermons are found in the parables of Jesus, so sermons are found in His miracles. Through these miracles you can discover great spiritual truths He is revealing for you.

22

FEEDING THE FIVE THOUSAND

Scripture passage: John 6:1-14

After these things Jesus went over the Sea of Galilee, which is the Sea of Tiberias. Then a great multitude followed Him, because they saw His signs which He performed on those who were diseased. And Jesus went up on the mountain, and there He sat with His disciples. Now the Passover, a feast of the Jews, was near.

Then Jesus lifted up His eyes, and seeing a great multitude coming toward Him, He said to Philip, "Where shall we buy bread, that these may eat?" But this He said to test him, for He Himself knew what He would do.

Philip answered Him, "Two hundred denarii worth of bread is not sufficient for them, that every one of them may have a little."

One of His disciples, Andrew, Simon Peter's brother, said to Him, "There is a lad here who has five barley loaves and two small fish, but what are they among so many?"

Then Jesus said, "Make the people sit down." Now there was much grass in the place. So the men sat down, in number about five thousand. And Jesus took the loaves, and when He had given thanks He distributed them to the disciples, and the disciples to those sitting down; and likewise of the fish, as much as they wanted.

So when they were filled, He said to His disciples, "Gather up the fragments that remain, so that nothing is lost." Therefore they gathered them up, and filled twelve baskets with the fragments of the five barley loaves which were left over by those who had eaten.

Then those men, when they had seen the sign that Jesus did, said, "This is truly the Prophet who is to come into the world."

Key verse: "There is a lad here" (v. 9).

Weary in body and mind, Jesus withdrew into the mountains for a quiet time with His disciples. But when the people discovered His whereabouts, they immediately thronged to the spot, so that when Jesus lifted up His eyes, He found a great multitude gathered around Him. In spite of His physical exhaustion, when Jesus saw the people as sheep without a shepherd, He had compassion on them. All day long He preached the Word to them and healed the sick among them.

Then evening drew nigh. The people were without food in a desert place. There were no restaurants nearby, no trees with fruit, no bushes with berries. What was to be done?

Then Andrew came to Jesus and said, "There is a lad here who has five barley loaves and two small fish, but what are they among so many?" The boy and his lunch here become the focal point of the story.

I can imagine the little fellow starting out from home in the morning toward the mountains. He had heard much about the Man from Galilee and was anxious to see and hear Him. Like all thoughtful mothers, his mother prepared a nice lunch for him in case he got hungry along the way. So with lunch bag thrown over his shoulder, and carrying a stick in one hand, he slowly made his way up the mountainside.

After a walk of an hour or so, he suddenly found himself on a plateau in the hills, and there before him was a great crowd of people. He was too short to look over the heads of the people, so he didn't know what was going on—but slowly he nudged his way through the huge crowd until finally he found himself right near the disciples and the Master.

All day long his eyes were fastened on this wonderful Man. He hung onto every word He uttered. He was too interested to remember to eat his lunch, so when evening came, it was still intact. Perhaps the biggest miracle of this whole incident was the fact that the young lad had not already eaten his lunch!

When discussion about food took place between Jesus and His disciples, the little fellow stood nearby and listened to every word. Then he suddenly remembered the little lunch his mother had so carefully wrapped up for him. He tugged at the coat of one of the disciples and said in an eager voice, "Mister, I have some lunch with me—five loaves and two fish. I'll be glad to give them to Jesus. Please tell Him He can have my lunch."

Andrew relayed the message to Jesus. Jesus took the loaves and fish, blessed them, and then distributed them among the people through the hands of His disciples. In a miraculous way He fed the 5,000 who had gathered so that all were satisfied, and 12 basketfuls of the fragments remained.

What are the spiritual lessons in this story?

The Master needs human instruments. It was quite possible for Jesus to have turned the stones on the hillside into bread and feed the people, but He chose to use what was available. Jesus has chosen to build His kingdom and carry out His work in this world through human instruments. He needs you and me. If the spiritually hungry people of this world are to be fed, it will be only through men and women who will place themselves, with their talents and capabilities, at the disposal of the Master and allow Him to work through them.

At the end of World War II a number of American soldiers came upon a little chapel that had been seriously damaged in the conflict. Among the ruins they found a beautiful statue of Christ that had been broken into several pieces. Carefully they gathered together the broken segments and skillfully put them back together. But to their disappointment, they could not find the hands of the statue. For some time they were at a loss to know what to do, but finally they decided simply to put the statue back where it had apparently stood originally. Underneath they carved this inscription: *He has no hands but yours.*

How true this is! Jesus has no hands but ours, no feet or eyes or voices but ours. He needs us to reach down and lift up the fallen. He needs us to proclaim the message of deliverance and redemption. He needs us to walk into the ghettos and villages to minister to needy people.

We may not have much, but the Master wants what we have. The young lad had only five loaves and two fish. Andrew asked Jesus, "What are these among so many?" But Jesus did not turn down the young boy's gift. He received it gladly and made wonderful use of it. In like manner, what we have to offer to Jesus may not be much, but nevertheless Jesus will never refuse it. And however small the talent or gift may be, He always has use for it. The question is not "What do I have?" but "Am I willing to give what I have?" It's not "What can I do?" but "What can Christ do through me?"

Notice that the young boy gave his all. It's very easy to imagine him saying to himself, "If I give all of my lunch, what will I have for myself? I'm just as hungry as the others, and it's a long walk back home. I'll keep two loaves and a fish for myself and give the rest to Jesus." The boy could have done this very easily, and we would not have blamed him for it. But he chose to give all he had to Jesus, and he did it willingly—no one forced him to do so.

Jesus wants our all; our talents, our possessions, our skills, our service, our bodies as a living sacrifice. Are we willing to turn over everything into His hands?

In the hands of Jesus, our little becomes much. The lad had only five loaves and two fish, and there were 5,000 people to be fed. But the glorious fact is that in the hands of Jesus the little lunch became a mighty feast and was sufficient for the needs of all. The account tells us that the people had "as much as they wanted . . . they were filled." More than that, there were 12 basketfuls of bread and fish left over!

What we have to offer to Jesus may not be much. But He will take it, bless it, break it, and use it to the satisfaction of hundreds of hungry hearts. The story of the gospel is not so much an account of how God has used people of unusual ability but how He has used people of ordinary ability in a most extraordinary and miraculous way. Jesus has the glorious knack of taking some little thing and making a mighty instrument of it.

So don't say to yourself, "I'm too young for service," or "I don't have much to offer." Just hand over what you have, and you'll be amazed how God will use you and your talents in His service.

A well-known poem describes an auction that was taking place one day. The last item the auctioneer held up was an old, dusty, battered violin. He asked, "What am I bid for this violin?" One man offered a dollar, another two, and another three. Then out from the crowd stepped an old, white-haired man who took the violin from the hands of the auctioneer, carefully wiped off the dust, tuned up the strings, and then began to play. Soon the place echoed with beautiful strains of violin music. The men stood motionless. The women wiped tears from their eyes. Never had they heard such beautiful and inspiring music.

When the old man finished, without a word he handed back the violin, and once again the auctioneer called out, "What am I bid for this violin?" This time the bidding was swift and spirited. "One hundred dollars—two hundred—three hundred." And the old violin, which had been on the verge of being sold for a paltry sum, now went to the highest bidder for $300.

When our seemingly worthless talents and lives are placed into the hands of the Master, they're suddenly transformed into something of real beauty and value and become instruments of blessing and salvation to many. The touch of the Master's hand makes all the difference.

Happily, the lad chose to surrender the little he had (the fish and the bread) to the Lord and thereby became a partner with Him in ministering to the needs of thousands of others. How happy he must have been as he related the miracle to his parents that evening when he got home! We can imagine how his eyes sparkled as he said, "Mom, Dad—Jesus and I fed them all!"

God needs you today. Surrender to Him all that you have and are. And He will bless you and use you mightily in His service for His glory and the good of others.

23

HEALING THE WITHERED HAND

Scripture passage: Mark 3:1-7

> And He entered the synagogue again, and a man was there who had a withered hand. And they watched Him closely, whether He would heal him on the Sabbath, so that they might accuse Him. And He said to the man who had the withered hand, "Step forward."
>
> And He said to them, "Is it lawful on the Sabbath to do good or to do evil, to save life or to kill?" But they kept silent.
>
> So when He had looked around at them with anger, being grieved by the hardness of their hearts, He said to the man, "Stretch out your hand." And he stretched it out, and his hand was restored as whole as the other. Then the Pharisees went out and immediately plotted with the Herodians against Him, how they might destroy Him.
>
> But Jesus withdrew with His disciples to the sea. And a great multitude from Galilee followed Him, and from Judea.

Key verse: "Stretch out your hand" (v. 5).

Picture this drama in your mind. It's the Sabbath day, and the scene is a Jewish synagogue. On one side you have the Pharisees, and on the other side Jesus. In the middle is a man with a withered hand. They're all in the synagogue on the Sabbath for the same purpose—to worship God and listen to the exposition of the sacred Scriptures. But what a difference in spirit and behavior!

Let us look at this narrative from several different angles.

The condition our Lord confronted. Note: "A man was there who had a withered hand." Where? In the synagogue, the house of worship.

Substitute the word "church," and you'll have the situation we're faced with today. Some people attend church and participate in the worship service and take the name of Christ upon their lips—but their hands are withered and ineffective.

This man's hand had not always been worthless. A correct translation from the Greek would read, "whose hand had *become* withered." Time was when he had a strong hand. With that hand he labored and made his living. Luke tells us that it was his right hand; tradition says he was a mason by trade. Now his hand is paralyzed, useless.

In the Scriptures the hand has some interesting suggestions associated with it:

Luke 9:62—"No one, having put his *hand to the plow,* and looking back, is fit for the kingdom of God" (emphasis added). Here "hand" speaks of the useful labor of service. The hand of service can become a withered hand. All the aggressiveness has gone. Here is a person who was once keen for the kingdom of God, eager to serve, winning others to discipleship. But now this person has lost his or her first love; the zest for service is gone; the enthusiasm has died out in the heart. Or perhaps the *attractiveness* of his or her service is gone.

A withered hand is an ugly thing, an awkward thing, a bungling thing. We need to be winsome and gracious in our service. Some people do good awkwardly, with no graciousness of touch. They are too severe, lacking in compassion, with no real sympathy for others. Many need a kindly touch.

1 Tim. 2:8—"I desire therefore that the men pray everywhere, *lifting up holy hands*" (emphasis added). Here the hand is a symbol of prayer. What happens when the vitality goes out of our prayer life? What happens when we become irregular, undisciplined, in our prayer life? Has your prayer life become dull and dead? Real prayer is power; empty prayer is a farce.

Gal. 2:9—"They gave me and Barnabas the *right hand of fellowship*" (emphasis added). Here the extended hand speaks of confidence, love, concern, communion. What about your hand of fellowship with other persons? Is it a firm, strong, loving hand? Or is it a withered hand? Have you had some misunderstanding with someone, failed to set things right, and then withdrawn the hand of fellowship?

Is the Lord speaking to you about a withered hand today? A withered hand of *service?* A withered hand of *prayer?* Or a withered hand of *fellowship?*

The compassion our Lord displayed. Note the difference in the attitude of Jesus and then the Pharisees toward the man with the withered hand. Jesus saw him as a person in need, while the Pharisees saw him as an object of contention. Jesus looked upon him with love and compassion; the others had no concern for him whatsoever. The record tells us that Jesus was grieved at the hardness of their hearts.

Then note the difference in attitude toward the Sabbath. The Pharisees had a very legalistic and narrow concept of the Sabbath as a day of taboos and prohibitions. To them religion was a matter of rituals, rules, and regulations. As a result, they were more concerned about keeping the Law than helping a needy person. On the other hand, Jesus believed that acts of mercy and necessity were lawful on the Sabbath. To Him religion was not Law, but service—it was love for God and love for people. So Jesus felt the man was more important than the rules.

The pharisaical spirit is still alive today in persons who carry out all the external acts of religion but have no compassion for suffering people and never reach out to help them.

The command our Lord gave. It was a twofold command: "Step forward" and "Stretch out your hand."

Step forward—Jesus spoke directly to the man with the withered hand. Our individuality is often lost in the crowd, but Christ deals with us only as individuals. Our communication is effective when people react by saying, "This is God speaking to *me.*" The Spirit of God does speak to you. He knows who you are, where you live, your background, your condition.

This was a difficult command. J. B. Phillips, well-known Bible translator, translates it like this: "Stand up and come out here in front!" Here was a public invitation that was not easy. It was bad enough to have a withered hand and be sitting in the congregation, but it was worse to come up before the whole crowd. Jesus sometimes asks the difficult thing to shatter our pride. We cannot insist that this is the only method one should use, but the whole New Testament is on the side of openness in our confession of Jesus Christ.

Stretch out your hand. Again this was a difficult command. The man's hand was paralyzed; how could he stretch it out? So much depended on the mental attitude of the man. If he looked at the hand, he would say, "It is impossible; I have not moved this hand for years." If he looked away from the hand into the face of Jesus, then it would seem possible.

No matter how withered your hand has become, Christ wants to heal it. He wants to heal the useless hand of service, the paralyzed hand of prayer, the withdrawn hand of fellowship.

The consequences that Christ produced. What happened to the hand? Here's what it became:

A healed hand. It became once again a strong, effective hand. The man could move it; he could use it.

In the Old Testament we have a wonderful illustration of a healed hand. Look at Moses in the Book of Exodus. He tried to lighten the load of the Jews, but he had a withered hand, withered in the hot fires of an uncontrolled temper. In an attempt to rescue a fellow Israelite from an Egyptian overseer who was flogging him mercilessly, he struck and killed the Egyptian. Therefore Moses was forced to flee the country. For 40 years he was laid aside. Then God healed that withered hand and gave him a new commission. Moses went back to Egypt and became the emancipator. With that hand he directed his people through the Red Sea and led them out of bondage.

In the New Testament we also have a good illustration. Look at Peter in John 18:10-11. He had a withered hand, withered by self-assertiveness and self-confidence. On the night of Christ's arrest, he whipped out his sword and cut off the ear of the servant of the high priest. Jesus rebuked him: "Peter, you must not defend Me with methods like that." His hand was later healed, and he was restored to fellowship and filled with the Holy Spirit. He became one of the greatest Christian leaders of the Early Church. With that healed hand he reached out and lifted up a man lame from birth and restored him to health and strength.

A helping hand. The man's hand was healed, not for exhibit, but for work. We can't imagine for a minute that the man wrapped his hand up in silk and showed it off on special occasions, saying, "Have you seen my healed hand?" Certainly not. He put it right to work. The next day he appeared at the employment agency to look for a job. Christ heals us, not to make us ornaments, but *instruments*.

A humbling hand. His healed hand reminded the man that if it hadn't been for Jesus, this hand would still be paralyzed and useless. There was no room for boasting, self-glorying, or self-confidence. There was room only for gratitude and thanksgiving.

John Robertson, famous preacher in Glasgow, Scotland, had a very effective ministry. But then he met with defeat in his personal life.

Filled with discouragement and drained of power, he said to God, "I want to *resign.*"

The Spirit within said, "I want to *re-sign* your commission."

He was restored in mind and heart, and the remaining years of his life became the richest of his ministry.

24

HEALING THE PARALYTIC

Scripture passage: Mark 2:1-12

Again He entered Capernaum after some days, and it was heard that He was in the house. Immediately many gathered together, so that there was no longer room to receive them, not even near the door. And He preached the word to them. Then they came to Him, bringing a paralytic who was carried by four men. And when they could not come near Him because of the crowd, they uncovered the roof where He was. And when they had broken through, they let down the bed on which the paralytic was lying. When Jesus saw their faith, He said to the paralytic, "Son, your sins are forgiven you."

But some of the scribes were sitting there and reasoning in their hearts, "Why does this Man speak blasphemies like this? Who can forgive sins but God alone?"

And immediately, when Jesus perceived in His spirit that they reasoned thus within themselves, He said to them, "Why do you reason about these things in your hearts? Which is easier, to say to the paralytic, 'Your sins are forgiven you,' or to say, 'Arise, take up your bed and walk'? But that you may know that the Son of Man has power on earth to forgive sins" —He said to the paralytic, "I say to you, arise, take up your bed, and go your way to your house." And immediately he arose, took up the bed, and went out in the presence of them all, so that all were amazed and glorified God, saying, "We never saw anything like this!"

Key verse: "Arise, take up your bed, and go to your house" (v. 11).

139

This account of the paralytic who was brought to Jesus for His healing touch is a story with tense action and deep emotion. It is both fascinating and instructive. Read the text carefully to get all the details, and then apply the lessons learned to your heart and life.

Notice some unusual points about this incident:

Four men carried one man. "They came to Him, bringing a paralytic who was carried by four men." It was necessary that the man be brought, for Jesus was his only help and hope. He was so paralyzed that he could not come by his own strength. Note the "four." This is the correct number to bear a litter for some distance with a man upon it. If one of the four had not shown up to carry one corner, or if he carried it falteringly, then bringing this man would have been hindered. If two or three of the four had let him down, the sick man would not have been brought at all. The bringing was the good work of the *four* men. They were concerned about the paralytic, they had confidence in the love and power of Jesus, and they *cooperated* in bringing him to the Master. Possibly they had met Jesus before or had seen Him heal. So they told this man, persuaded him, and brought him to the Lord.

All around us everywhere are "sick" men and women, boys and girls. They are sick in sin and neglect and are in need. They need Jesus. They may not even know who can help them, but if you believe Jesus is the Son of God, then you know. It is your responsibility to bring them to Christ.

Bringing people to Jesus is the greatest business in all the world and the most satisfying. Merton S. Rice, great Methodist preacher of Detroit, once said, "The moments I have been closest to Christ were when I had a concern for some lost person."

He went in through the roof and came out through the door. When the four men, with the paralytic, got to the house where Jesus was preaching, they were not able to get through the door. Too many people crowded around Him. But nothing could stop them—they had started the job and were determined to see it through. So they climbed up onto the roof and removed enough tiles to make a large opening. Part of the crowd must have craned their necks in astonishment to see the sky appearing right through the roof. The four men paid no attention to the concern of the crowd. They proceeded to tie ropes to the four corners of the man's thin mattress, partially folded the man and mattress together, and let the bundle down—right in front of the Master himself.

Many obstacles had stood in their way to accomplish this feat. First was the *crowd,* selfishly jamming the doorway, blocking the way. They wouldn't move over and let a needy man get to Christ; they didn't care whether or not he got to Jesus. They were unconcerned, selfish, and a hindrance. Many people are like that today.

Custom hindered the four men also. The usual way to get into a house was to come in through the door. But seeing that this was quite unachievable, they did it the "impossible" way and came through the roof.

Critics hindered them too. Though they came to hear Jesus, it was only to find fault with Him. "After all," they thought, "no one can forgive sins except God. This man is blaspheming in God's sight."

In spite of the *crowd, custom,* and *critics,* the paralyzed man was healed. He was dropped in through the roof and swept past them all on his way out the door.

We need a dynamic and persistent faith. We can't let roofs or people stand in the way. We need to come into the presence of the Great Physician ourselves and bring others to Him too.

He came in on his bed and went out with his bed *on him.* The four men brought him believing and therefore receiving. Notice: "When Jesus saw *their* faith" (emphasis added). Whose faith? The faith of the four men who carried the litter, and the faith of the paralytic himself. It was a *combined* faith and a *persistent* faith.

We don't know how long the poor man had been lying on that bed—perhaps many years. He was completely enslaved to it. But what a glorious deliverance was his! Notice the word "immediately"—that's the way Jesus worked. No pills, no injections, no bed rest, no gradual recuperation, but an instantaneous, miraculous healing. A paralytic no more! He jumped off of that prison bed, rolled it up, slung it over his shoulder, and pushed past the gawking gang to energetic freedom. No doubt his friends, temporarily forgetting their obligation to fix the roof, jumped down and with him praised the Lord all the way home.

I have found no greater joy in the world than bringing a needy friend to Christ, and seeing him or her walk away forgiven and delivered. Try it yourself!

25

HEALING THE DEMONIAC

Scripture passage: Mark 5:1-20

Then they came to the other side of the sea, to the country of the Gadarenes. And when He had come out of the boat, immediately there met Him out of the tombs a man with an unclean spirit, who had his dwelling among the tombs; and no one could bind him, not even with chains, because he had often been bound with shackles and chains. And the chains had been pulled apart by him, and the shackles broken in pieces; neither could anyone tame him. And always, night and day, he was in the mountains and in the tombs, crying out and cutting himself with stones.

But when he saw Jesus from afar, he ran and worshiped Him. And he cried out with a loud voice and said, "What have I to do with You, Jesus, Son of the Most High God? I implore You by God that You do not torment me." For He said to him, "Come out of the man, unclean spirit!"

Then He asked him, "What is your name?"

And he answered, saying, "My name is Legion; for we are many." And he begged Him earnestly that He would not send them out of the country.

Now a large herd of swine was feeding there near the mountains. And all the demons begged Him, saying, "Send us to the swine, that we may enter them." And at once Jesus gave them permission. Then the unclean spirits went out and entered the swine (there were about two thousand); and the herd ran violently down the steep place into the sea, and drowned in the sea.

Now those who fed the swine fled, and they told it in the city and in the country. And they went out to see what it was that had happened. Then they came to Jesus, and saw the one who had been demon-possessed and had the legion, sitting and clothed and in his right mind. And they were afraid. And those who saw it told them how it happened to him who had been demon-possessed, and about the swine. Then they began to plead with Him to depart from their region.

And when He got into the boat, he who had been demon-possessed begged Him that he might be with Him. However, Jesus did not permit him, but said to him, "Go home to your friends, and tell them what great things the Lord has done for you, and how He has had compassion on you." And he departed and began to proclaim in Decapolis all that Jesus had done for him; and all marveled.

Key verse: "They . . . saw [the demoniac] sitting and clothed and in his right mind" (v. 15).

Through a variety of miracles Jesus demonstrated His power and authority over all things. He demonstrated His power over the human body by healing the sick and disabled—the leper, the blind, the deaf, the paralyzed. He portrayed His power over nature and the physical world by calming the storm on the Sea of Galilee and walking on its waters. By casting out evil spirits, Jesus proved His power over the spirit world and the human personality. By speaking the word of forgiveness and changing the character of individuals, Jesus confirmed His authority over sin and Satan. Let us not forget that the greatest miracle of all is not the healing of physical illness, but the transformation of a life—when a bad person becomes good, an impure person becomes pure, and a weak person becomes strong.

Healing the Gadarene demoniac is one of the most dramatic incidents in the ministry of our Lord. Here was a man sick in body, mind, and spirit, but the power of Christ completely delivered and transformed him—saving him from the "gutter most" to the uttermost!

The man. The picture the Gospel writer gives us of this man is one of abject wretchedness and degradation. The account tells us that he was "a man with an unclean spirit" and that he lived among the tombs. Like a wild man, he roved around the countryside naked, shouting at the top of his voice and intimidating everyone. People had tried to restrain him by binding him with chains, but he simply broke the shackles to pieces with his abnormal strength. He inflicted pain on himself by cutting his body with sharp stones. He was possessed not by just one but by many demonic spirits. Could anyone be more wretched?

In the New Testament the adjective "demonic" occurs about 55 times in the Gospels, and "unclean spirit" or "evil spirit" about 28 times. Some people claim that "spirit possession" is merely a figurative expression for moral depravity, or more definitely, for mental disease or insanity. But the New Testament clearly makes a difference between mental illness and spirit possession (see Matt. 4:24). According to the late Kurt Koch, German medico-psychologist, these two phenomena are characterized by a completely different set of symptoms. For example, if one prays for a mentally ill person, he or she will remain calm throughout. But a spirit-possessed person becomes upset and often violent.

"Spirit possession" describes the mysterious but real invasion and control of human personality by actual evil spirits of supernatural power. During my service in India, I witnessed several cases of this phenomenon. I have talked to missionaries from various countries who have also encountered numerous cases. In many instances exactly the same symptoms as described in the Gospels have been evident. In every instance, the authoritative command in the name of Jesus Christ has brought complete deliverance.

The Lord. The Gospel narrative so simply yet powerfully describes the transformation wrought by Christ in the personality of the demoniac. When Jesus entered the country of the Gadarenes (on the northern shore of the Sea of Galilee), the demoniac saw Him from a long way off, ran out to meet Him, and knelt down and worshiped Him. As depraved as the man was, he still had enough sense to recognize Jesus for who He was. Even the evil spirit within him recognized Jesus, for he cried out, "What have I to do with You, Jesus, Son of the Most High God? I implore you by God that You do not torment me."

Then with the voice of authority, Jesus spoke the word of deliverance: "Come out of the man, unclean spirit!"

What was the result? When the people of the countryside came upon the scene, they found the former demoniac "sitting and clothed and in his right mind." The *evil spirits* were gone; his spirit was free. No more raving and ranting; he sat calmly at the feet of Jesus. Ropes and chains were no longer necessary; he was in perfect control of himself. He no longer acted like a wild beast; he was now a liberated human being, a useful citizen. He left the tombs and went back home to his friends and told them all that the Lord had done for him. His witness was so astonishing and effective that "all marveled."

The pigs. One of the interesting sidelights of this miracle of deliv-

erance had to do with the herd of pigs into which Jesus commanded
the evil spirits to go. The pigs at once became so upset and violent that
they stampeded and ran down the mountainside into the sea and were
drowned—all 2,000 of them. When the owners of the pigs heard what
happened, they came to Jesus and begged him to "depart from their region."

What a contrast to the attitude of the former demoniac! He was so
excited and full of joy that he begged Jesus to allow him to stay with
Him. He wanted to bask in the presence of his Deliverer for the rest of
his life. Instead, Jesus told him to go and tell all his friends about it.

The owners of the pigs, however, wanted Jesus to get out of
town—and fast! They were much more concerned about the loss of
their pigs than about the deliverance of a helpless human being.

In the mountains of New Guinea live some of the most backward
tribes in the world. The people have recently been coming out of the
Stone Age. Someone has described their culture as a "pig culture."
Everyone raises pigs. The pig is part of the bride price when a young
man wants to marry. The pig is used as a sacrifice to appease evil spirits. Pigs are killed and eaten by the scores at the time of the annual
"sing-sing" festivals. People are so fond of pigs that they stroke them
like their own children. It used to be common for a woman to nurse a
baby pig if the pig's mother died suddenly.

A few years ago, a couple serving with Wycliffe Bible Translators
worked on the translation of the Gospels into one of the tribal lan-
guages of New Guinea. When they had completed their translation of
the story of the Gadarene demoniac, the missionaries gathered the
people and read to them that story in their own mother tongue. The
tribal people listened in rapt silence. One of the men spoke up as he
heard how Jesus ordered the evil spirits to enter the pigs and how the
herd ran into the sea and was drowned. He exclaimed incredulously,
"Two thousand pigs? You mean to say that Jesus thought a man was
worth more than *two thousand pigs?* But here a man is worth only *one*
pig!"

Primitive as these people might be, they had grasped the real significance of this story. The man was exactly right. Jesus *does* care more
for one person than for a whole herd of pigs. A person's redemption is
worth the whole world to Him. A delivered man is worth more than
tons of deviled ham!

The unchanging Christ. I will never forget my first encounter with spirit possession when I was a missionary in India. One Sunday morning I was sitting in the congregation of the Methodist church in Belgaum with my head bowed and my eyes closed during the pastoral prayer. Suddenly I felt a tap on my shoulder and looked up to see a village man standing there. He whispered to me, "Sir, I have brought my wife, who is possessed with an evil spirit. Please help us."

I was taken by surprise and whispered to him, "Sit down and wait until the worship service is over, and then I'll talk to you." But then I heard a commotion in the aisle and looked to see a woman on the floor, going through convulsions. I knew this would disturb the service, so I asked the man to pick up his wife and carry her to our missionary bungalow nearby.

As we sat on the stone floor on the veranda, I questioned the villager about his wife, and he told me that she had been possessed with an evil spirit for several months. He said that she often fell into the fire and hurt herself in various ways, and that the demon kept her from conceiving and bearing a child. All the people in the village were afraid of her because of the things she did, and so they would have nothing to do with her. The wife herself told me that the evil spirit often made her do things she didn't want to do.

I wasn't sure what to do. Was the woman really demon-possessed, or was she suffering from epilepsy and needed a doctor more than a minister? Then I remembered that several years ago I had heard a returned missionary from China lecture on the subject of demon possession. He had said that one sure way to distinguish spirit possession from any form of insanity was to ask the victim to speak the name of Jesus. If the person really had a demon, that demon would not allow him or her to utter the name of Christ or Jesus. So I decided to make the test.

I said to the woman, "Please say the name 'Yesu' [Jesus]." Immediately she was stricken dumb and could not say the name, even though she had easily answered my previous questions. I asked her three or four times to speak the name of Jesus, but each time she was unable to do it. So I decided it must be a genuine case of demon possession.

As I faced the situation, I felt so absolutely helpless. I prayed silently, "Lord, this is beyond me. You'll have to take over." Then God gave me the faith to act. I read from the Kanarese New Testament the story of Jesus healing the demoniac, made a few comments of encouragement, and then started to pray. Up until this time, the woman sat calmly, answering all my questions. But when I started to pray, she began to groan, her body started to jerk, and her eyes rolled wildly.

Then in a loud voice I cried out to the evil spirit, "In the name of Jesus Christ, the Son of God, I command you to come out of this woman!"

At these words, the woman fell forward from a cross-legged sitting position, and her forehead hit the stone floor like the crack of a pistol shot. Her feet, still crossed, were stiff and sticking up behind her. Again I said, "In the name of Jesus Christ, the Son of God, I command you to come out of her!"

Suddenly she rolled over and sat up calmly. Her eyes were no longer wild; she had a look of utmost calm on her face, and her body had stopped shaking.

I said to the woman, "Say the name 'Yesu.'"

She said clearly, "Yesu."

I said, "Say *Yesu Kristanu* [Jesus Christ]."

She repeated it.

I said, "Say, 'Jesus Christ has delivered me.'" (Of course, this was in her own language.)

She repeated, "Jesus Christ has delivered me."

Then I remembered the parable that Jesus told about an evil spirit that was driven out of a house, but when he came back and found the house swept and empty, he brought seven other spirits with him, "and the last state of that man is worse than the first" (see Luke 11:23-26). So I explained to the woman that the evil spirit was gone, but her heart was now empty, and she needed to invite Christ to come into her heart and take charge. She then prayed and accepted Christ into her life. I gave her a New Testament. She could not read, but her husband said he could and that he would read it to her. I told her she must go home and witness to all the people what God had done for her.

The next Sunday morning I was in the same situation. I was seated in the worship service, with head bowed and eyes closed during the pastoral prayer. Suddenly I felt a tap on my shoulder. I looked up to see the same village man who had brought his wife the previous Sunday. I must confess that I thought, "I hope the evil spirit hasn't come back to his wife."

But imagine my joy when he whispered to me, "Sir, I have brought my wife. She has been completely delivered and has been telling people about Jesus. She wants you to baptize her, and I would like to be baptized also." They were both standing there, smiling.

Usually when people are converted, we give them a period of training before baptizing them, but this case was so unusual, and the people so radiant, that at the close of the morning service, I told this woman's story to the whole congregation and baptized her then and there, and her husband too.

A few weeks later this couple again came into Belgaum, bringing with them this time another woman who, they said, also had a devil and she wanted to be prayed with and baptized. Mr. Reddy, the pastor, and I prayed with the woman, then baptized her. During the baptismal ceremony, she suddenly started to violently shake and tremble, but the ceremony went ahead—"I baptize you in the name of the Father, Son, and Holy Ghost." The woman became quiet.

I often visited that village afterward and found that these two illiterate but truly transformed women were wonderful witnesses to what Christ can do. They testified to everyone in the village, and they are living witnesses.

I know that Jesus is the same yesterday, today, and forever. He is still speaking through His Word today; He is still healing and delivering people; He is still speaking the word of forgiveness and transforming people. He is the Son of God, the Friend of sinners, the Savior of the world, our coming King.

Praise God! We belong to an *unchanging Christ* and an *unshakable Kingdom!*

Epilogue

Our spiritual trek has been an exciting adventure, because we have meditated on the most exciting Person who ever lived. Christ has been the chief Actor, occupying center stage in this, the greatest drama in all of human history. In His birth, He became our Brother; in His life, our Teacher and Example; in His death, our Redeemer; in His resurrection, our Conqueror; and in His second coming He is our Hope. Now He is the all-sufficient One; He is all things to all people.

To the astronomer, He is the bright and morning Star.

To the architect, He is the chief Cornerstone.

To the builder, He is the sure Foundation.

To the baker, He is the living Bread.

To the banker, He is the hidden Treasure.

To the biologist, He is the Life.

To the carpenter, He is the Door.

To the doctor, He is the great Physician.

To the florist, He is the Lily of the Valley, the Rose of Sharon.

To the geologist, He is the Rock of Ages.

To the jeweler, He is the Pearl of Great Price.

To the judge, He is the Judge of all nations.

To the king, He is the Lord of the universe.

To the lawyer, He is the Advocate.

To the newspaper reporter, He is the good tidings of great joy.

To the philosopher, He is the Truth.

To the philanthropist, He is the unspeakable Gift.

To the scientist, He is the Creator.

To the student, He is the great Teacher.

To the traveler, He is the Way.

To the sinner, He is the Lamb of God, who takes away the sin of the world.

Praise be to God for the gift of His Son!